China's Coming
War with Asia

China's Coming War with Asia

Jonathan Holslag

Polity

First published in 2015 by Polity Press
Reprinted 2015

Polity Press
65 Bridge Street
Cambridge CB2 1UR, UK

Polity Press
350 Main Street
Malden, MA 02148, USA

ISBN-13: 978-0-7456-8824-4
ISBN-13: 978-0-7456-8825-1(pb)

A catalogue record for this book is available from the British Library.

Library of Congress Cataloging-in-Publication Data

Holslag, Jonathan, author.
  China's coming war with Asia / Jonathan Holslag.
    pages cm
  Includes bibliographical references.
    ISBN 978-0-7456-8824-4 (hardcover) – ISBN 978-0-7456-8825-1
  (pbk.) 1. China–Foreign relations–Asia. 2. Asia–Foreign
  relations–China. 3. National security–China. 4. National
  security–Asia. 5. China–Military policy. I. Title.
    DS33.4.C5H65 2015
    355'.033051–dc23
                  2014030399

Typeset in 11 on 13 pt Sabon
by Toppan Best-set Premedia Limited
Printed and bound in the USA by RR Donnelley

For further information on Polity, visit our website:
politybooks.com

Contents

Preface

When some of my colleagues in China and Europe read the manuscript of this book, they asked: Why this dramatic title? Honestly, I had my doubts too. I toyed, for instance, with less alarmist alternatives like "The impossible peace" or "Asia's China dilemma." But then, I thought, there is reason for concern, so why not be clear about it and make the argument boldly? Still, there are a few matters that I want to explain to readers in advance.

First of all, this book does not hold China responsible for the tensions that simmer in Asia. I do advance the argument that China's most important objectives are incompatible with the promise of a harmonious order, but several of these objectives are not necessarily more antagonizing than the ambitions of other powers and remain even fairly defensive. Moreover, many other powers had or have had similar aspirations, albeit in different contexts. I also show that Chinese diplomacy is about flexibility without compromise, but that too can be said about many other countries. The intransigence certainly does not have much to do with the quality of Chinese diplomats. This might have been so in the past, but I learned to appreciate most of today's officials as open-minded, inquisitive, hardworking, and very dedicated to the wellbeing of their country – probably much more than to the Communist Party. So, do not expect this work to be a diatribe against China. I consider China a normally rising country, entertaining normal ambitions, and facing the normal dilemmas of war and peace that so many other powers have grappled with in the past.

This book follows a structural approach in examining the strategic landscape in Asia. An important concept in this regard is the security dilemma. If one country tries to advance its security and gains power, that inevitably portends a loss of power and security for another. Economic ties, international organizations, and communication between countries, as this book also shows, can mitigate the security dilemma somewhat, but not sufficiently to prevent conflict if the power shift becomes very large. In the new Asian security dilemma, tensions are as much the consequence of China's rise as of the efforts of other powers, like Japan and the United States, to defend their military predominance, their privileged position in economic networks, and their status.

My warning of war does not imply that I take China's rise for granted. China is altering the regional balance of power, but it is still behind the United States. I find many of the recent euphoric treatises about China ill-informed and ill-judged. China's military capabilities have been modernized but are certainly not technologically superior. China's economy grows in size, but it remains dangerously unbalanced. Many decision makers I saw questioned the leadership's ability to redress this. The fierce anti-corruption campaign that President Xi Jinping unleashed at the time I was completing this book confirmed how daunting the domestic challenges are. China is a fragile power and so are the other Asian protagonists. This begs us to investigate which country is most able to address its shortcomings – or to make other countries pay for them. In the case of China, the sense of vulnerability partially explains its growing difficulties to strike a balance between its own interests and the concerns of its neighbours. China also does not need to become a new superpower to scare its neighbours. Even if China were to falter, history teaches us that rising powers that see their growth stagnate often become more nationalistic and dangerous. For a student of international politics, it is thus not only a task to assess how strong or vulnerable countries are but also how they deal with it.

I am fully aware that a book like this can come across as cynical: cynical because it seems to consider great power war as an inevitable tragedy, cynical also because it appears to minimize the progress made in our global society. I confess that I do not always feel comfortable with this myself and truly wish that I could be more optimistic. But if we really want to avoid another episode of major conflict, is it not better to go to the heart of the ugly new security dilemmas, face reality, and work harder to change it? All too often I have the impression that the optimists of this world too easily find satisfaction in superficial changes: broadening commerce, for instance, or dialogue, or some modest military exchanges. Even realists these days have difficulty in accepting that war becomes imaginable if their premises are applied to Asia. I remember several discussions with realists, where the majority of them offered a gloomy assessment, but rather unconvincingly jumped to the conclusion that things would still be alright. So, perhaps, the bleak prospect of war could be a stronger incentive than misleading optimism to tackle the pressing dilemmas, to make earnest efforts to solve territorial disputes, and to come up with an economic narrative that offers an alternative to the new destructive race for industry and natural resources. War in Asia has become more likely. Recognizing this should be the first serious step in any effort to prevent it.

Landen, 5 July 2014

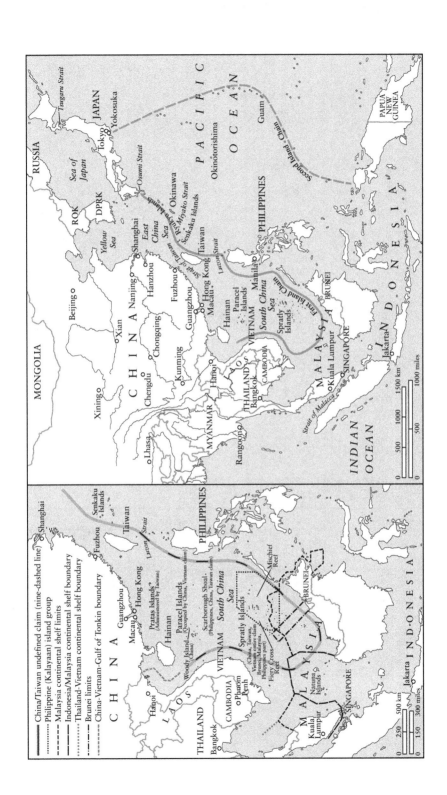

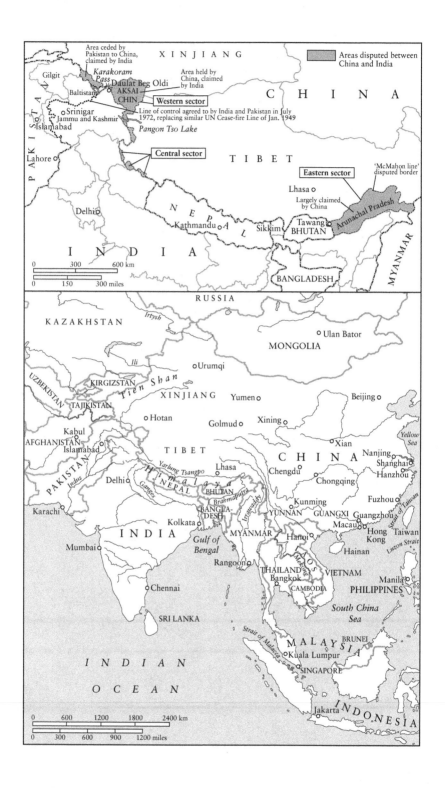

Areas disputed between China and India

Top map (Western/Central/Eastern sectors):

XINJIANG

Area ceded by Pakistan to China, claimed by India

Gilgit

Karakoram Pass

Baltistan

Daulat Beg Oldi

AKSAI CHIN

Area held by China, claimed by India

C H I N A

Western sector

Line of control agreed to by India and Pakistan in July 1972, replacing similar UN Cease-fire Line of Jan. 1949

Srinigar

Jammu and Kashmir

Islamabad

Pangon Tso Lake

Central sector

T I B E T

Lahore

'McMahon line' disputed border

Eastern sector

Delhi

Lhasa

N E P A L

Largely claimed by China

Arunachal Pradesh

Kathmandu

Sikkim

Tawang

BHUTAN

I N D I A

MYANMAR

| 0 | 300 | 600 km |
| 0 | 150 | 300 miles |

BANGLADESH

Bottom map (Asia):

RUSSIA

KAZAKHSTAN

Irtysh

Ili

Ulan Bator

MONGOLIA

Tien Shan

Urumqi

KIRGIZSTAN

UZBEKISTAN

TAJIKISTAN

XINJIANG

Yumen

Beijing

Kabul

AFGHANISTAN

Islamabad

Hotan

Golmud

Xining

Xian

Nanjing

Yellow Sea

Shanghai

Hanzhou

Indus

PAKISTAN

TIBET

Yarlung Tsangpo

Lhasa

Chengdu

C H I N A

Chongqing

Delhi

Ganges

NEPAL

Himalaya

BHUTAN

Brahmaputra

BANGLA-DESH

Kolkata

Irrawaddy

Kunming

YUNNAN

GUANGXI

Fuzhou

Guangzhou

Macau

Hong Kong

Taiwan

Strait of Taiwan

Karachi

Mumbai

I N D I A

MYANMAR

Hanoi

Hainan

Luzon Strait

Gulf of Bengal

Rangoon

LAOS

Mekong

THAILAND

Bangkok

VIETNAM

Manila

CAMBODIA

PHILIPPINES

Chennai

South China Sea

SRI LANKA

Strait of Malacca

MALAYSIA

BRUNEI

Kuala Lumpur

SINGAPORE

I N D I A N

O C E A N

Jakarta

I N D O N E S I A

| 0 | 600 | 1200 | 1800 | 2400 km |
| 0 | 300 | 600 | 900 | 1200 miles |

– 1 –

Asia's China Dilemma

"I just cannot understand why half the world is blaming us. Our growth benefits all our neighboring countries. We have come to work with regional organizations and have offered to develop disputed waters together," the Chinese academic gesticulated passionately. "I think we can find solutions for most of our problems, but then our neighbors should not call the United States in to make us do this at gun point. Our claims are reasonable, you see, no one should exploit tensions to complicate China's rise."[1] It was an amicable discussion, the academic, an Indonesian official, and myself, sipping soda water during an oppressive afternoon on the green banks of Symphony Lake. We were taking a break from the Shangri-La Dialogue, the annual security gathering in Singapore, where senior Chinese delegates also found themselves in a crossfire of allegations and responded with a very similar indignation. I find this one of the intriguing aspects of China's rise, the fact that Chinese insiders – from the young think-tanker to the senior politician – all seem to believe sincerely that their country is not to blame for tensions in Asia and that China has shown a great deal of flexibility to adjust itself to the wishes of its neighbors, to establish dialogues, and to avoid armed conflict. Knowing many of them for several years, I have no reason to question their sincerity, but the dilemma remains: as much as neighboring countries believe that China has to make more concessions, China believes that it has already done enough and that other major powers are playing up the anxiety in its neighborhood.

Great Aspirations

This book aims to clarify this dilemma. Its main argument is that China's important interests, its great aspirations as I call them, are incompatible with the idea of a peaceful rise in a complex Asian environment. In other words, China's strategic objectives are irreconcilable with those of its neighbors and that other Pacific juggernaut, the United States. This is a bold statement and it has to stand against several fine studies that arrived at completely different conclusions – or at similar observations with arguments that failed to withstand closer scrutiny. Let me first explain how I make my case in this book, so that the next section can explain how it differs from other works. To start with, it is important to make sense of the apparent changes in China's behavior in the past six decades. One can, after all, not just forecast conflict without explaining the ostensible tendency of China to be more cooperative and to integrate in the global order. Throughout the first four chapters, I reconstruct how China indeed came to show more military restraint toward its neighbors and how its leaders came to emphasize economic interests and the idea of a mutually beneficial division of labor to advance peace along its borders. They reveal how these leaders piloted the country gradually into more and more regional organizations, took more initiative in developing these organizations, and became deft practitioners of dialogue. Moreover, foreign policy became increasingly diffuse with Beijing allowing provinces, companies, and other actors to play a more autonomous role in the broadening of

relations with other countries. These chapters also eluci-
date the important changes in discourses and thinking
about international affairs, the remarkable shift from Mao
Zedong's struggle to the current paradigm of peaceful
development. All that seems thus to confirm that the optimistic students of China's rise have it right: the country
has moved from belligerence to moderation and can hence
be expected to integrate peacefully in the global order.

But change does not mean adjustment. As the next step
in building my case, I posit that the apparent modifications
of China's foreign policy are misleading. This is for two
reasons. On the one hand, as the first chapters reveal, it
was usually not China adjusting its behavior that paved
the way for cooperation. In fact, the other Asian protagonists adjusted first. When China stumbled into the Cultural
Revolution, for instance, it was Japan that kept the communication lines open. Later on, it was the United States
that spearheaded rapprochement by means of Henry Kissinger's secret diplomacy. The consequent diplomatic revolution led to overtures by Southeast Asian countries and a
rapprochement with South Korea. The Soviet problem
solved itself. In the 1980s, ASEAN invited China to participate in trade fairs and later on in more political dialogue. It was thus not China's changing foreign policy that
sparked the improvement of its security environment.
Instead, it was the changing security environment that
allowed China to improve its image. On the other hand,
as will become clear, China could improve its image
without making compromises on its great aspirations, its
pursuit of wealth, power, and security. China has proved
remarkably adept in minimizing resistance against four
aspirations. These two points come as important correc-
tives to the predominant idea of a proactive grand strategy
of opening up and compromise.

This is followed by a third argument. China's great
aspirations, the book asserts, are inevitably revisionist. In
other words, China does aim at a very fundamental transition of the distribution of power and, hence, a transition

of the global order. How can we know? Not by looking at China's current behavior. Contrary to what optimists argue, China's stance toward international rules and organizations is no reliable indicator of whether it is a revisionist or status quo power. Even its stance on territorial expansion is not a good guide. Instead, revisionism is about power. One does not need to challenge the rules or the territorial status quo to work toward the revision of the international order. But it is true, of course, that *if* China gains so much power that it finds itself at the top of a new international order, it can be expected to shape rules and borders to its advantage. China is a revisionist power because its first great aspiration, control over frontier lands like Tibet and Xinjiang, entails its command over the world's largest combined natural and demographic resources. Its second great aspiration, to defend the position of the Communist Party by making China a high-income economy, implies that it will become the largest economy in the world, be in the best position to shape relations with other countries to its advantage, and have the greatest resources to spend on military capabilities. Its third great aspiration, the recovery of lost territory, like Taiwan and the islands in the South China Sea, can only result in a huge strategic advantage over the other regional powers. The fulfillment of China's core objectives are thus destined to upset the international order and, especially with India failing to reform, to establish something that will have all the characteristics of a new empire: a new sinocentric empire.

From a Chinese viewpoint these aspirations are reasonable, defensive, and just. But these interests and the search for security portend nothing less than a power-maximizing strategy that is incompatible with both the security interests of neighboring countries and the privileges of the leaders of today's global order. We should not expect this security dilemma to diminish. The last three chapters show that China is by no means satisfied with its progress so far and that it will try to push ahead with its economic and military expansion. But we do not know whether it can succeed. Domestic and external challenges will become increasingly pressing. This, the book contends, can lead to three kinds of conflicts. First there is the prospect of a traditional hegemonic war, the kind of war famously described in Robert Gilpin's *War and Change in World Politics*. In that case the United States, unwilling to give up its privileges and to be dominated, will be locked in an armed conflict with its main challenger. This is the most straightforward scenario. But China is still lagging far behind the United States in terms of military power and the quality of its economy, so that hegemonic war should not be expected any time soon. Second, there is the possibility of a regional war. Even if China has a long way to go to catch up with the United States, it does increasingly overshadow the lesser powers in its neighborhood, threatening their sovereignty, and challenging their prosperity. China still has the advantage, the last chapter posits, that its neighbors are divided by geography, history, and economic interests, but with some of them all the ingredients for conflict are present: a contested border, a history of discord, economic competition, fear about China's military capabilities, and nationalism. This applies especially to Japan, Vietnam, and India. The multitude of territorial disputes in a climate of growing nationalism could trigger regional armed conflicts. These can also pull in the United States so that a regional conflict escalates into a "premature" hegemonic war. Even if the United States is not directly threatened, it has signed several security treaties with the parties involved and the prospect of a Chinese victory over its neighbors will only aggravate the fear of its rise in the longer run. A third scenario is that of a faltering power. In that case, China's economic growth would stall and prevent it from fulfilling its great aspirations. In this case, the threat does not emanate from China's rise, but from the insecurity experienced by the Chinese leadership and its tendency to rally domestic support by diverting attention to external threats. The book does not

consider the option of collapse and retreat. Yes, the Ming
Emperors burned their ships in the past, but given the vast
overseas interests and the victory of new modes of trans-
portation over physical barriers, this cannot be repeated
in today's world.

These three options instantly overcome the traditional
divide in the debate between scholars who believe that
China will be more assertive as it becomes more powerful
and others who assume that China will not fight because
it remains so impotent. But there is more. The shift in
thinking and discourse, which I spoke of earlier, the shift
towards a paradigm of peace, could even aggravate the
security dilemma. Both China and the other powers assume
that justice is on their side. Chinese officials genuinely
believe that their country has shown a remarkable degree
of restraint and has made great efforts to avoid conflicts.
They believe also that China has made important economic gestures and, of course, that Chinese entitlements
to disputed bits of territory, including Taiwan, are perfectly justifiable. In fact, China is convinced that it works
towards a restoration of justice and the ending of the
unfair privileges that other powers acquired in their imperial past. But China's great aspirations are of course all
about replacing one empire with another and other countries in the region certainly do not consider China's interpretation of mutually beneficial cooperation, freedom of
navigation, and political harmony to be very fair. So, even
if their decision makers have been socialized with the
imperatives of defense, restraint, and fairness, this is by no
means enough to avoid violence. That again stands as an
important corrective of the more positive constructivist
ideas that have been en vogue in the debate about China's
ascent.

The main aim of this book is thus to present a sophisticated explanation for the growing tensions in Asia and
to address some of the starry misconceptions. Besides that,
it also comes as an update of the economic, political, and
military power plays in the region. While the first chapters

provide an indispensable historical account of China's rise in Asia, the last chapters offer new insights into the contemporary dilemmas. They draw from a large number of recent interviews, field visits, and data to demonstrate that China is by no means a satisfied power. The book is written for a broad readership of students with an interest in international politics and decision makers. To the latter, it offers one important piece of advice: stop pretending that conflicts can be overcome if they cannot be solved. It makes no sense to insist that peace can be maintained if no party is prepared to compromise on core interests. For that reason, the cautious statesman better anticipates yet another episode of major international turbulence, turbulence that could well spill over into other parts of the world and, indeed, into other spheres, like cyber and space. If those statesmen really want to go into the history books as true peacemakers, this treatise advises them to move beyond an obsession with confidence building, dialogue, and economic interdependence. These apparent mitigating factors can even be counterproductive, because they distract attention from the fundamental conflicts and convince different parties that previous efforts to promote exchanges put justice on their side.

Power Shift or Paradigm Shift

So, how then does this work relate to the many existing excellent studies on China's rise? To begin with it comes as a critique of those scholars and decision makers who have presented China's rise in Asia more as a paradigm shift than a power shift. What matters, their argument goes, is not that China is becoming stronger, but that it is committed to using its newly gained strength to the benefit of the region and to steering clear of the sort of aggressive behavior that other powers displayed in the past. By pursuing peaceful development, China should stand as an exception against a long turbulent history of great power wars and will inevitably change the very nature of international power politics. There are different ways to look at the promise of a peaceful rise. Chinese leaders like to argue that the world has changed in a fundamental way, so that ideas have to change in a fundamental way too. "Peace and development are the underlying trends of the world," Premier Li Keqiang asserted. "China's new government will...more firmly and effectively build a community of common destiny to share peace and prosperity."[2] In his study about China's new diplomacy, Zhiqun Zhu concluded that it does not follow a particular diplomatic model, but incessantly searches for a new one, creating a new identity while practicing it, reforming itself, and changing undesirable policies.[3] One of the foremost conduits through which China's identity as an international actor has changed is through membership of international organizations. As Harvard's Alistair Ian Johnston put it: there are still tensions between realpolitik and idealpolitik in China's foreign policy, but multilateralism has become the predominant ideational construct behind China's foreign policy.[4] But there has also been a lot of trial and error domestically. Environmental problems, for instance, or pandemics, have made officials increasingly recognize that their country is part of a global village.[5] Likewise, the growing global presence of companies has reshaped the perspective of decision makers away from the national interest to the international marketplace.[6] Another interesting thesis is that diplomats, after a series of incidents with neighboring countries, have learned that old-fashioned power politics is not useful for China and that it therefore has to replace the Western anarchic logic of international politics with its tributary traditions.[7]

But China's worldview, as many scholars have signaled, remains too distrustful to speak of a deep reconstruction of ideas and identities. Instead, its policies of peaceful rise can be considered the outcome more of a functional appreciation of China's growing interconnectedness with other economies and of the fact that its economic development

needs stability. China needs trade to grow and peace to
trade. The baseline in this regard is that China has too
much to lose from belligerent behavior. Expansionism no
longer pays off and any aggression would derail China's
growth. Growing dependence on trade has also created
greater vulnerability. China now depends enormously on
other countries for safe maritime trade, stable financial
markets, and clear economic rules. The incentive to coop-
erate is thus huge. That cooperation also has become more
institutionalized. While China understands that regional
organizations can constrain its maneuverability, it also
grasps that there is no way back, that it should learn to
use these bodies to advance its own agenda peacefully, and
that aggressive unilateralism can turn them against China.[8]
Furthermore, as a more competitive trading nation, China
itself increasingly has an interest to promote an open economic order, free trade, and solid guidelines for international commerce. There is also a cooperative spillover
into the realm of security. Because of China's globalizing
security interests, it has a stake in international security
cooperation. "China should be a responsible power,"
writes Peking University's Wang Yizhou, "and assume a
greater part of the burden in international security cooperation."[9] Yet, economic interdependence is no cast-iron
guarantee of peace. As David Rapkin and William Thompson remarked, "Though it may constrain conflict escalation processes, interdependence also generates serious
economic frictions that can easily offset or overwhelm its
conflict-suppressing effects."[10]

Liberal trade-motivated peace makes sense for an emerging trading nation. Yet, students of China's rise have demonstrated that commerce has not entirely wiped out the
fixation with security, borders, and armed force. From this
viewpoint, peaceful rise could still be the best way for
China to achieve security. Defensive realists recognize that
conflicts remain, but that the Chinese government is not
seeking to overthrow the international system and understands that aggression would come at an enormous cost.

Tang Shiping, a professor at Fudan University, makes this case forcefully. "While China may become more powerful, it is unlikely that it will use its newly gained power to intentionally threaten other states," he argues. "If there is a security dilemma between China and another state, two genuine defensive realist states can find a way to signal their true benign intentions and work out their differences." Whereas Tang attributes this posture mainly to the diplomatic lessons learned under Deng Xiaoping, others maintain that it is vulnerability that dictates China to be defensive. Andrew Nathan and Andrew Scobell, two seasoned China watchers, posit: "The main tasks of Chinese foreign policy are still defensive: to blunt destabilizing influences from abroad, to avoid territorial losses, to moderate the suspicions of surrounding states, and to create conditions that will sustain economic growth."[11] In *Partial Power*, an important work on contemporary China, David Shambaugh argues: "Chinese diplomacy remains remarkably risk-averse and guided by narrow national interests."[12] Important problems with defensive realism remain and proponents of this approach have largely failed to address two important critiques: intentions can change for the worse, and if restraint is a temporary product of weakness, it will also be abandoned as soon as China becomes more powerful.

It is here that we enter the more skeptical strands of international politics. Neoclassical realists insist that China cannot be trusted. China is not just a state that craves power; it is an authoritarian state that craves power. That makes a difference. If Asia comes to be dominated by an authoritarian China, the prospect for liberal reform in any of its non-democratic neighbors will be greatly diminished, writes Princeton's Aaron Friedberg. Even the region's established democracies could find themselves inhibited. With its enhanced global reach and influence, China would be able to more effectively support non-democratic regimes and to present some variant of its own internal arrangements as a viable alternative to the liberal democratic capitalism of the West.[13] It comes as no surprise to neoclassical realists that a country like China wants to maximize its power; it is even encouraged to do so by the unequal international order. It will also use its power to influence international politics as soon as it feels confident enough. The one thing, however, that makes this particularly problematic is thus its domestic political system. That makes China almost pre-programmed to crush the existing liberal world order as soon as it has the means to do so. Scholars like Friedberg do their best not to look like China bashers, but what flows from this approach inevitably looks a lot like a clash between good and bad. The cause of the conflict is structural; the real threat is Chinese politics, its dictatorship, its state capitalism, its nationalism, its imperial tradition, and – worse – its militarism.

Offensive realists share that skepticism. The unequal structure of international politics forces a major developing country like China to try to revise that global order and thus to challenge the leading countries. The desire for power is always present and the leading countries show daily how it works. Revisionism just needs the right opportunity to become successful, a technological breakthrough, an efficient economic model, or a mistake by the ruling powers. Offensive realists refute, however, that domestic politics and ideology make a significant difference. In the case of China, its government just does what every other government of a major developing country would have done if it had its opportunity, which is to maximize its power and to try to become a hegemon. As long as the risk of defeat looms, they keep quiet and show restraint, but as soon as they gain dominance, they will no longer refrain from using their clout coercively. No one has made this claim more forcefully than John Mearsheimer: "China will want to make sure that it is so powerful that no state in Asia has the wherewithal to threaten it. It is unlikely that China will pursue military superiority so that it can go on the warpath and conquer other countries in the region, although that is always a possibility," he wrote. "A much more powerful China can also be expected to try to push the United States out of the Asia-Pacific region, much the way the United States pushed the European great powers out of the Western Hemisphere in the 19th century."[14] Even though few Chinese scholars of international politics want to portray their country as the next Asian hegemon, some of them make prescriptions along the lines of offensive realism.

I believe that the offensive realists have it right about China's rise. It was pretty clear to me that neoclassical realism did not make much sense. One could, after all, perfectly imagine that a successful China would swap its mercantilism for free trade and adopt some sort of democracy, yet still confront the other powers with the same security dilemmas. Neither is there a reason to assume that a democratic China would suddenly attach less importance to the reclaiming of so-called lost territory. Until a few years ago, I considered China's foreign policy to hover somewhere between defensive realism and interdependence liberalism. It was often hard not to fall for the arguments of officials that restraint was the only possibility for China to survive. "It is geopolitics that disciplines us," said an official at the international department of the Communist Party. "If we were to act aggressively against one country, we would have problems with all twenty neighbors." Its desire to get back some of the territory it has lost does not really change that. Many of its claims are as valid or problematic as the claims from other countries. With the United States snooping in its maritime fringes, China's naval modernization seemed equally qualified as a defensive effort. Furthermore, Chinese decision makers seemed genuinely convinced that their country had to support an open global economic order and that its state capitalism had to make place for a real market economy – step by step, of course, as happened with other rising powers. Likewise, China became heavily involved in international organizations and got gradually more interested in the preservation of the global commons. Nobody can deny also that more and more Chinese scholars shifted their attention away from traditional power politics to issues like international law, public diplomacy, and soft power. But, still, important doubts remained.

Two unmistakable flaws in the arguments of the realist optimists struck me. On the one hand, they have not been able to dismiss the criticism that China will become more assertive when it gets more powerful and that its gains in power will prompt others to resist it. It is of course true that the country is still fragile today and so it makes sense to display restraint. The moment when China's capabilities will overtake those of the United States is still far off, if it arrives at all. So is the moment that Robert Gilpin's power transition theory describes as a systemic crisis. Yet, even if it is not yet a mature power, China's economic and military power will soon eclipse that of its neighbors, which could lower the threshold for using coercion. Even partial powers can become bullies. China seeks to enhance its security through power and China's gains in power compromise the security of its neighbors. This security dilemma becomes ever more pressing as the balance of power shifts. It can prompt bolder balancing and increase the chance that incidents escalate or spiral out of control. On the other hand, and this is related, optimists build their case on an assessment of China's recent behavior in regard to international rules and organizations. There is no denying that the People's Republic has become very interested and active in multilateral cooperation, but this remains selective. It does not prefer multilateralism addressing maritime disputes, for example. Restraint on this crucial issue leaves us to grapple with the counterargument of skeptics that China will resort to unilateralism to enforce its claims as soon as it is powerful enough. But there is more, even in the realm of low politics, as it is uncertain whether multilateral cooperation will be durable. This is not only because of China's role, but equally because other powers might come to find multilateralism less useful if

Beijing gets the clout to advance interests that oppose theirs.

That brings us to another major shortcoming. Like the neoclassical realists, the optimists make their case essentially by focusing on China and explaining how China affects the international order. But they fail to analyze how the international order affects China and shapes its preferences. A structural approach to China's rise is key for different reasons. First, it helps us to understand how the international order has influenced what China aspires to. With the United States as the leader of the existing order, China largely wants what the United States has. Domestically, progress is identified with consumerism, consumerism with high incomes, high incomes with competitive industries, and competitive industries with technological innovation. Externally, progress is measured by the ability to protect sovereignty, the ability to follow the United States in generating force along the entire spectrum of high-tech war, the ability to shape international trade, the ability to shape international rules, and to be revered as a strong nation. Second, it draws our attention to the fact that the existing structure of international politics prevents China from achieving all this. Third, it makes us face the reality that the only way it can be successful is by maximizing its power and by changing the structure of international politics. Security and power maximization are two sides of the same coin. Fourth, it forces us to recognize that if China becomes successful in engendering such a transformation at the structural level, it will end the privileges of the strong and render the weak more prone to exploitation. The structural approach implies thus that there is no reason to blame the revisionist, because its aspirations are often no less understandable than the claims of the incumbent leading nations, and its policies no less destabilizing than those of the current leaders when they were in the ascendant. Neither is there much difference whether this happens by maintaining the existing international rules or not. The outcome is the same and means that other countries will be less able to fulfill their interests, if only because the success of the new power creates new desires. These are thus exactly the arguments that offensive realists put forward. In fact, a careful read of the initial work of John Mearsheimer on China, disregarding the perceptions that his outspoken personality has often created, reveals offensive realism as a very dispassionate framework for analyzing China's rise. What ultimately made me shift towards offensive realism were not the claims that China had become more assertive. China's confrontational response to North Korean muscle flexing and tensions in disputed waters around 2010 were, after all, also the consequence of more assertive posturing of the United States and its partners. Instead, it was a series of research projects on more specific topics – like China's military transition, its role in regional organizations, and its economic policy – that pointed me to an important conclusion: whatever Chinese leaders claimed in terms of their grand strategy of peace for Asia, these concrete policies can only work if China effectively builds a new empire and is able to shape the sovereign decisions of its neighbors. It seemed unlikely that these policies would be changed. It is even more unlikely that countries like Japan, India, Vietnam, and the United States would accept the consequent regional order. At the same time, an exploration of the imperial trajectory of great powers in the past clarified how rising powers succeeded by gradually hardening their regional influence in the wake of private pioneers and failed if they did so too fast. That imperial trajectory clarified how powers diffusely and often even unintentionally transit from defensive to offensive policies. It also drew my attention to one important missing element in offensive realism: rising powers resort more easily to aggression, not when they are successful, but when they fail.

China's rise is of course interesting enough in its own right, but the following chapters will also provide insight into some of the broader debates about international politics. I will posit, for example, that a country like China has no choice but to be revisionist. The status quo is not an option. National interests are not preordained, but there is no reason to expect China to forgo its ambitions to have its citizens become as rich as those in developed countries, control over its frontier land, and the reunification of the motherland. Settling for anything less could spell the end of the leadership of the Communist Party and, indeed, the end of the People's Republic as it exists today. China needs to change the international order because the current distribution of powers does not allow China to fulfill its interests. If the concept of revisionism is used properly it helps us to understand a lot of the tensions caused by China's ascent. Revisionism, as I mentioned before, does not equal territorial expansion, aggression, or the wish to wreck the existing rules and organizations. Revisionism, in essence, is the desire to change the distribution of economic power, and that can happen perfectly well within the prevailing norms. But, contrary to what neoclassical realists assume, that does not make the challenge to other countries less severe.

This is closely related to the discussion about multilateralism. China came to use Asian regional organizations to build confidence with its neighbors. It is clear that Chinese officials became more familiar with the rules of multilateral cooperation and picked up some of the proposals that smaller countries tabled in these regional meetings. Yet, multilateralism remains a form of power politics by different means. It has to be considered a form of brinkmanship. Great powers trade a degree of obedience for acceptance, legitimacy, and influence. Once in place, it can serve as an important instrument to reassure smaller countries, as a disguise for bilateral negotiations, and as a channel to promote their standards. Powers like China also try to advance their own vehicles for regional cooperation, parallel with the existing ones. Besides revisionism and multilateralism, China's relations with Asia also reveal a lot about the growing sophistication of economic nationalism. China's contemporary economic nationalism is not a matter of resisting globalization and not even of narrow mercantilism that is fixated with the balance of payment. China's economic nationalism is about manipulating economic globalization, diverting the lucrative parts of international trade, shaping international technical standards, and positioning its companies strategically along the global and regional supply chains. China's rise thus shows that power politics has certainly become more refined, but it also leaves us with one of the most important sources of concern: no one can tell us whether that sophistication will last.

— 2 —

The Revolutionary Overture

Ravaged, hungry, and tired: that was the state of China when Mao Zedong proclaimed it a Republic of the People in 1949.[1] Out of a population of 540 million, 110 million citizens in the south fearfully awaited the final showdown of the civil war that had raged for over 20 years between Communists and Kuomintang Nationalists.[2] The other 430 million grappled with the old plague of poverty and a new political reality. Decades of war had battered down the average life expectancy in the rural villages to a mere 35 years, destroyed their irrigation canals, and decimated a large part of the livestock. Barely one third of Chinese farmers owned an ox to till the land.[3] The Communists had brought land reform, ridding peasants of the crippling feudal system of the Kuomintang, but also came with inquisitive Party cadres, new laws, and taxes to lower food prices in the cities. Most of these cities had given Mao the benefit of the doubt, but inflation, hunger, and unemployment made patience wear thin. The factories in Manchuria were shattered during the war and partially dismantled by the Soviets.[4] What remained of the crucial plants around Shanghai, after the bloody siege on the Nationalists, was relocated to the hinterland to be farther from the imperialists and closer to the mines. About three million city dwellers were forced to move with it.[5] "Wherever there is life here," wrote one of China's renowned novelists, "there is struggle."[6] No wonder that the Chinese people craved for peace.

The Four Great Aspirations

But however much the people wanted peace, Mao wanted power first. It is true that many Chinese leaders recognized the need for stability. Mao himself remarked: "The most important question at the present time is the question of establishing peace. China needs a period of three to five years of peace, which would be used to bring the economy back to pre-war levels." Prime Minister Zhou Enlai echoed: "If we do not focus on production, what shall we rely on to support the military campaign and the consolidation of our victory? Production is the basic task of our new China. If we do not have food to eat, we will not be able to do anything else at all."[7] Yet, peace was also deceiving. Communist ideology held that true peace would be hard to achieve. Mao himself in this regard recited Vladimir Lenin, arguing that struggle ceaselessly destroys one relative condition for another relative condition and that peace only means that struggle has temporarily become less acute. It is known that Mao entertained a vision of perpetual peace, but also assumed that peace had to be based on harmony and that China's conception of harmony would be resisted by the leading powers. Besides ideological reasons, China had ample practical reasons to be skeptical. Mao loathed the prospect of a peace in which villagers would retreat back into their petty lives without building a strong state around the leadership of the Communist Party. He rejected peace if that would turn China once more into a backward prey for economic exploitation and unequal exchanges. He also denounced peace if it permitted the major powers to dominate China's neighborhood. What mattered was thus not the peace itself, but the conditions of the peace.

Power was the prerequisite for a beneficial peace. It does not demand much imagination to understand how that concern and sense of insecurity came about. For the band of leaders that had moved from over two decades of guerrilla fighting into the quiet courtyards of Zhongnanhai, the walled compound next to the Forbidden City, the world outside remained a frightening place. In the winter of 1949, Mao could still discern on his map many vestiges of the Kuomintang, in the current provinces of Yunnan, Chengdu, Guangxi, on a range of islands off the Chinese coast, on Hainan, and, of course, on Taiwan, which would remain a bulwark of resistance in the decades to come. From those islands, the nationalists continued to raid the mainland and its maritime supply lines. In the south was the restive area of Tibet. The remote west, the unruly region of Xinjiang where the Eastern Turkestan Movement operated, continued to be exploited by the Soviets via joint-stock companies, mining concessions, railways, and unequal trade schemes, together with other places like Inner Mongolia, Manchuria, and Port Arthur.[8] By 1950, the People's Republic had asserted its formal control over most of these areas, but resistance was rife. The more Mao's regime advanced, the more its northern neighbor insisted on obedience. The other imperial power, meanwhile, roamed in a large part of its periphery. The United States had deployed about 8,000 troops in South Korea, kept 13,000 soldiers in Japan, developed military facilities on Okinawa, maintained military advisors on Formosa, and expanded its Pacific Fleet with an additional aircraft carrier.[9] Back in Washington, politicians bickered about whether to contain China or to destabilize it. In Southeast Asia, France maintained 120,000 troops close to the border with China to keep the "Reds" out of Indochina. Paris had agreed with Washington and London not to recognize China as long as it was needed to keep it in check.[10]

China had thus to pursue a project of nation building in an uncertain context. That nation building rested on four great aspirations. First of all, it implied securing control over frontier lands, Yunnan, Tibet, Xinjiang, Inner Mongolia, and so forth. Second, it meant that the Party had to be recognized as the legitimate political structure. It was clear for its leadership that this required bringing back stability, feeding the people, and enabling sustained economic growth. Third, China had to be able to get its sovereignty respected: on paper through diplomatic recognition and in practice by resisting great power interference. Fourth, a strong Chinese nation had to recover its lost territory. As Mao famously put it during the Civil War: "We the Chinese nation have the spirit to fight the enemy to the last drop of our blood, the determination to recover our lost territory by our own efforts, and the ability to stand on our own feet in the family of nations."[11] After 1949, the main focus was on Taiwan. The so-called reunification of Taiwan and a few other islands controlled by the Kuomintang became a "sacred task" of the leadership. But China also insisted on regaining some parts on the disputed border with India. In 1954, the Indian Prime Minister, Jawaharlal Nehru, much against the will of other politicians, recognized Tibet as a part of China. Two years later, Zhou Enlai told Nehru that he could live with most of the McMahon Line, the border as it was demarcated between Imperial China and British India in the Simla Accord of 1904, but only after equal negotiations, which Delhi refused. From then onwards, the two sides remained locked in conflict. Non-recognition of the two largest sections, today called Aksai Chin and Arunachal Pradesh, is largely symbolic. China does not really expect to recover Arunachal and India entertains no serious hopes for getting back Aksai Chin, but several smaller sections have been disputed more earnestly, like Tawang, Bomdi La, and Daulat Beg Oldi. China also took an interest in the islands of the South China Sea. When Japan renounced its claims on the Paracel or Xisha Islands, the Spratly or Nansha

Islands, and the Pratas or Dongsha Islands, China was quick to assert "inviolate sovereignty." Zhou Enlai also endorsed the nine-dashed line, which extended China's territorial claim on most of the South China Sea, and signed the 1958 Declaration on Territorial Waters, which formally demanded the return of the three island groups.[12] It took more time for Beijing to assert its sovereignty over the East China Sea. The Senkaku or Diaoyu islands had been under Japan's control since 1895, but China denounced the San Francisco Treaty of 1951 by which they were put under American administration. Only in 1958 was a first claim made and that was restated only after oil was found in the East China Sea in 1969. In 1970, China argued for the first time that it had preeminent rights on the continental shelf, which at some places extends over 300 miles from China's coast and ends less than 150 miles from Japan's Okinawa.

From China's perspective, these four great aspirations were reasonable and just. The emphasis was on rebuilding and defending the country, not on offense and aggrandizement. If there was already a revisionist power, then, China insisted, it was the United States, which badgered the region with its warships, unlawfully put troops in many strategic places, and made one incursion after another with its fighter jets. The Soviet Union was not much better, but this could not be said publicly until the late 1950s. That leads us to the most important repercussion of China's four great aspirations: if it was to fulfill its project of nation building in this precarious environment, it needed to break the dominance of the superpowers and to restore its position as the most powerful polity in Asia. That China wanted to undermine the power of the United States and the Soviet Union was clear. Already in 1937, Mao pronounced the objective to create a new world order that would restrain the influence of the leading powers, and this has continued to run as a red line through China's foreign policy ever since.[13] In the 1950s, this would be embedded in Zhou Enlai's Five Principles of Peaceful Coexistence:

respect for territorial integrity and sovereignty, non-aggression, non-interference, equality and mutual benefit, and peaceful coexistence. In the 1970s, Mao captured his plans for a new international order in his Three Worlds Theory. The third world and the second world had to join forces to restrain the two superpowers of the first world. To the Chinese leadership this implied a restoration of fairness in international politics, to end their privilege to exploit weaker countries, to halt their interference with domestic affairs of others, and to obtain respect for states with different development trajectories. Again, from a Chinese viewpoint and arguably even from an ethical viewpoint, many of these objects were very legitimate, but the precondition to advance this agenda was, again, a redistribution of capabilities between states and thus a major shift in the balance of power.

Less explicit was the aim to become the largest power in Asia. Formally, the Chinese leadership denied that it strove towards hegemony or a new empire and stressed that it wanted all the socialist countries to become more prosperous at the same time. Yet, the creation of a new Chinese empire, at the geopolitical heart of Asia, was the logical outcome of several operational objectives. The effort to integrate all Chinese frontier lands, like Tibet and Xinjiang, around the traditional coastal center, meant the creation of a nation with the most impressive combined resources for state power in Asia in terms of demography, land, agriculture, minerals, and freshwater. The objective to attain the same level of industrial production and technological innovation, which was sketched out already in 1950, implied that China would become the largest economic power globally and regionally – leaving India as the only possible challenger. The reunification of Taiwan and the recovery of lost territory by all possible means implied that China had to have the military resources to deter and defeat its neighbors and the United States – eventually also in an alliance formation. The desire to create a secure neighborhood presupposed the capacity to shape the preferences of neighboring governments and to dissuade them from inviting other great powers to be present. The only way for China to work toward all these goals was, inevitably, to become the most powerful country in Asia. That brings us back to the bedrock assumption of China's strategic thinking: no beneficial peace without power. In the same vein, there could be no beneficial peace without Chinese primacy in Asia.

If one puts oneself in the shoes of the Chinese leaders at that time, it was evident that the regional order had to be revised and that the only way to do so successfully was to maximize the country's power. That does not mean that such revisionist objectives made China the belligerent spoiler. Beijing's territorial ambitions, for instance, were not necessarily less reasonable than those of Japan, Vietnam, or India. With their historical maps, archaeological discoveries, geographic interpretations, and knowledge of the evolving international conventions, they could all make reasonable claims, reasonable claims that made compromise without losing face very difficult. Nor was it so bizarre that China harnessed its military capabilities to prevent the two superpowers from encroaching on its borders, to deter them from meddling with China's efforts to recover lost territory, and, in the long run, to break through America's security perimeter. It is even less difficult to imagine why China had to become the largest economic power. If one considers the Chinese income per capita to be the same as Japan's in 1950, the Chinese economy would be seven times bigger than that of Japan and four times bigger than that of the United States. With such wealth, the need for raw materials would be vast and, equally so, the repercussions for the overall regional balance of power. China has been a revisionist power by default, if not out of sheer necessity. Any other power with such complex domestic conditions and so disadvantageous an international order would probably try to achieve the same.

Primacy, however, remained a distant dream. The more instant concern was to keep the country together without selling it out to the superpowers for some illusive form of peace. Throughout the first two decades, this would turn the revisionist ambitions into a protracted guerrilla campaign, this time not so much aimed against the enemy within, but against rivals outside. That new guerrilla campaign had several mutually reinforcing objectives. To begin with, it needed to keep the Chinese society mobilized. If the People's Liberation Army was downsized from 5 million troops in 1949 to 3 million troops in 1953, the People's militia was expanded from 5 to 22 million troops, whose primary responsibility was to assist in the country's reconstruction.[14] The rest of the population was called upon to participate in collective farming and new state-owned industries. Another target was to maintain the Party's leadership, which was pursued through the promotion of benefits to the people, personal cult, nationalism, administrative control, and a host of common adversaries. China also had to strive toward economic independence, initially by searching pragmatically for economic opportunities in Moscow and some European capitals, later on through stringent strategies of autarchy. Furthermore, China wanted to strengthen its political autonomy with regard to the United States and the Soviet Union.[15] In less than a decade, this would lead China into a conflict with both giants and most of its smaller neighbors.

Leaning on One Side

China's first policy was to lean on one side, the Soviet side. This was not at all self-evident. On the one hand, Beijing was still well aware that Moscow had refused to support the Chinese Communists in picking up the gauntlet against the Kuomintang until 1946. Mao himself confided: "It would be just as wrong for China to rely only on the

Soviets and snub the United States and Britain." China was deeply disturbed about Russia's privileges on Chinese soil. "Some people in the democratic parties, students, and workers discuss the question of the presence of Soviet troops, the independence of Outer Mongolia, and the removal of mechanical equipment from Manchuria by the Soviet Union," Government Chairman Liu Shaoqi added. That was even before Mao's humiliating visit to Moscow in the winter of 1949. Stalin initially even refused to see him and kept him under lock and key in an icy dacha.[16] "He let me stay there for two months without negotiations," Mao later recorded, "so finally I got mad and said that if he did not want to negotiate I would go home." On the other hand, the Party did not want to close the door to the United States either. "We also have trade relations with the imperialists," Zhou Enlai stated in a conversation with the Albanian Foreign Minister. "In fact, we may do even more trade with the countries that have revisionists at their helm, but this must be done on the basis of the principle of equality."[17] A cable from December 1949, for example, enthusiastically stated: "Besides the Soviet Union, there are more states that are on the eve of having trade relations with us... Britain, Japan, the United States, India, and other states are already doing business with us or will soon being doing so."[18] Furthermore, although the Chinese probably did not know everything about the internal debates in Washington, they should have known from interventions by President Harry Truman and Secretary of State Dean Acheson that not everyone was opposing cooperation with the Reds or trying to derail them. By the beginning of 1950, President Truman had started to backpedal on helping the Kuomintang and to prepare the withdrawal of troops from South Korea. The defensive perimeter that the Secretary of State spoke about did include Japan, the Ryukyu Islands and the Philippines, but not Formosa or the Korean Peninsula.

The ultimate decision to swing to the Soviets has been the subject of long debate. After all, China could also have decided to hedge between Moscow and Washington. Ideology, better communication lines, and existing cooperation certainly influenced China's choice for the Soviet Union. Strategically, also, it seemed more dangerous to antagonize a close and omnipresent neighbor than a remote empire that lurked on the maritime fringes. Even if there is no clear evidence from the archives, there can be no doubt that Russia, not the United States, was an important threat and that the choice for leaning on one side, as Mao called it, was temporary and had to allow China to stand on its own feet in the longer run.[19] If pragmatism was the foundation of the alliance with the Soviets, there was a combination of elements that explained the hostility towards the Americans. First, China probably did not know enough about how divided Washington was regarding how to handle China and especially that the option of a rapprochement was still left open. Second, the support for the Kuomintang had a decisive impact on public perceptions of the United States and made it a tempting adversary for the political elite. A Chinese professor explains this very neatly in Derk Bodde's intriguing Peking diary of 1949. "At one time America apparently wanted a genuinely progressive government in China. During the past two or three years, however, it has seemed to be interested less and less in liberalism and more and more in anything, no matter how reactionary, that might be a bulwark between it and communism," the academic observed. "This change has coincided with growing reaction within the Chinese government itself. The result is an American government, which talks constantly about democratic rights, yet continued to aid a Chinese government increasingly mindless of these rights. That is why we Chinese have become anti-American. We are not against the American people but against the American government."[20] This was further facilitated by a third factor: ideology. Finally, the American intervention in Korea presented itself, albeit illusively, as an important opportunity for China to gain leverage in the partnership with the Soviets, to deter further American interference in China's neighborhood, and for Mao to strengthen his personal leadership.[21]

The Korean War froze the fault lines of the Cold War in Asia and estranged China further from the United States. The decision to deploy over a million American troops was Mao's own, as he reportedly acknowledged. "One man and a half decided on the Korean intervention."[22] Many Party members opposed the intervention. "Fight, fight, fight. We have been fighting over several decades in the past. People now want peace," asserted Marshal Lin Biao. "It is utterly against the people's will to engage in more fighting. Our nation has just been liberated, the domestic economy is a great mess, the army's equipment is still to be updated. How can we afford more war? Besides, we could be pretty confident fighting the Kuomintang, yet to fight the modern American army equipped with atom bombs is quite another matter."[23] Gao Gang, another Politburo Member, confirmed: "Our land has been through over 20 years of war. We have only just been united and a sense of peace has to be restored. If we fight again, I am afraid our economy will not be able to bear the strain. Fighting war is not all fists, it's money."[24] There were important strategic reasons to go to war. Once the North Korean leader Kim Il-Sung had persuaded Stalin of the need to attack the South, Stalin encouraged or at the very least approved China's intervention.[25] The Chinese decision was almost certainly influenced by suspicion of the United States. In January 1950, Washington had announced the discontinuation of its support for the Kuomintang, but by June of that year it had reversed that decision. Fearful that Taiwan, called an unsinkable aircraft carrier by General MacArthur, would fall, pushed by the Taiwan lobby in Congress, and alarmed by the North Korean offensive of June, it resumed its aid to Taiwan and sent the Seventh Fleet into the Taiwan Strait.[26]

In August, United States forces not only violated China's air space, but General MacArthur also paid a visit to Taiwan, publicly stating that appeasement of China was a flawed strategy.[27] That month, Mao already warned that: "If the US imperialists won the war, they would become more arrogant and threaten us." General Wu Hsiu-chuan, who intervened in the UN Security Council on behalf of China, summarized the dilemma even more cannily: "Suppose a detachment of the armed forces of a country hostile to the United States were to occupy Hawaii, while another detachment of the same country was attacking the neighbor of the United States, Mexico. Suppose the aggressor then assured the American people: Our troops will not commit any aggression. Is it conceivable that the American people would believe in these assurances?"[28] As American troops moved northwards, Beijing started issuing sterner warnings that an invasion of North Korea would cause China to intervene. On October 1, the Allied troops crossed the 38th parallel. Chinese troops moved in a few days later. Defense and deterrence were thus certainly important. But it is unlikely that Mao's instruction to go to war was entirely the result of calculations about the security environment. However risky it was, war could prove an opportunity for him to consolidate his leadership. Mao also understood that the request of Joseph Stalin to intervene would strengthen his leverage toward Moscow in negotiations about military assistance, easier access to financial aid, and support for China's industrial plans.[29]

After the armistice of 1953, Beijing publicly rationalized the immense human sacrifices with the idea of preventing a domino effect that threatened to strangle the new Chinese regime in its cradle. "By using the bases in Japan, the United States inherited the adventurism of the Japanese militarists, following the history since the war of 1895 and took the track of conquering China," Zhou Enlai claimed. "They wanted to calm China first and after occupying North Korea they would come to attack China."[30] At the same time, however, Mao stated that the United States had become so embroiled in the Cold War in Europe and so overstretched that a protracted war with China had become very unfavorable.[31] As a result, China gradually turned to another important component of its revisionism: the construction of a strong industry as the firm foundation of China's power.[32] What China had in mind for the long run was obvious: to join the ranks of leading powers and therefore to establish a strong economic base. China wanted a new economic order in which the imperialist powers ceased their economic privileges and in which it became a leading industrial and technological powerhouse itself. China's obsession with economic power was the consequence of a very anarchic view of the global economy. It reckoned that a strong government needed a strong economy to secure popular support and consequently to prevent other powers from sowing dissent. "If we cannot resolve economic problems, if we cannot build modern industry, and if we cannot develop productive power, then the common people will not necessarily support us."[33] Economic strength was also needed to preserve independence and to gain bargaining power. "Our nation has obtained political independence, but if our nation wants to achieve complete independence, the completion of industrialization is necessary," Mao and Zhou asserted. "If the industry is not developed, a country may become the other country's vassal...Should we let the USSR develop heavy industries and national defense industries, and let our nation develop light industries? Can we do that? In my opinion we cannot do that."[34] Furthermore, economic power was considered the basis of military strength: "Without industry there can be no solid national defense, no well-being for the people, no strength for the nation."[35]

Recovery

Industrialization became the backbone of China's first Five-Year Plan (1953–7). About 70 percent of investment was allocated to the development of new factories, mines, and other infrastructure. At that point, 20 percent of the heavy industry and 60 percent of the light industry was in private hands, but that period of "moderate capitalism" made way for state-controlled industrialization. This was not without success. The industrial output, steel production, and coal production grew by more than 15 percent each year. This coincided with a period of moderation in China's foreign policy and a search for stability. But the United States did not seem prepared to give that. Dwight Eisenhower had just become president, stating that the loss of China to the Communists was the greatest diplomatic defeat in the nation's history. Almost immediately he withdrew the Seventh Fleet from the Strait of Taiwan, so that the nationalists could deploy over 70,000 troops on the Quemoy and Matsu islands, about 15 kilometers from the City of Xiamen. Beijing responded with a shelling campaign, but sought to prevent escalation. The new Secretary of State, John Foster Dulles, backed by a vociferous chorus of China hawks in the Pentagon and in Congress, called for an assertive strategy in the Pacific. To let the Chinese get Quemoy and Matsu, he bristled, would enable the Communists to begin their objective of driving us out of the Western Pacific, right back to Hawaii and the United States.[36] Vice-President Richard Nixon advocated an Asian equivalent of the North Atlantic Treaty Organization (NATO) upon returning from his Asia trip, which would be followed by the creation of the Southeast Asia Treaty Organization (SEATO).[37] During the Korean War, defense agreements had already been signed: the mutual defense treaty with the Philippines in August 1951, the ANZUS Pact with Australia and New Zealand in September 1951, the San Francisco defense treaty with Japan, and, as the war came to an end, the mutual defense treaty with South Korea. Meanwhile, the United States started to provide vast funds to the French in Vietnam, started to provide aid to Laos and Cambodia, signed a defense treaty with the Philippines, sniffed out the possibility for supporting Burma, and threw its weight behind the Thai government. This was the containment strategy in action.

Already during the Korean War, China tried to find opportunities to improve its security environment. In 1952, Zhou Enlai explained in Moscow that China was aiming towards a regional strategy of exerting peaceful influence without sending armed forces.[38] That was followed by the Asia and Pacific Rim Peace Conference, which gathered delegates from 13 countries in Beijing's newly built Peace Hotel under banners with Picasso's famous peace dove. In 1954, China and India agreed on the Five Principles of Peaceful Existence. The same year, it grasped the Geneva Conference on Indochina as an opportunity to develop China's relations with the great powers, the Big Four, and to prevent the Western countries from ganging up against it. The Chinese delegation proposed to neutralize Vietnam, Cambodia, and Laos, and to prohibit alliances with these countries. "Our wish is that a restoration of peace will be realized in Indochina and that Laos and Cambodia will become peaceful, independent, friendly, and neutral countries. If they join America's alliances and establish American bases, then the restoration of peace becomes meaningless."[39] At the summit of non-aligned countries in the Indonesian City of Bandung, less than a year later, China vowed to enter into negotiations with Taipei and to relax tensions in the Far East, which received some praise among Asian countries. Said an Indian delegate: "As a result of the Bandung Conference, there is a lessening of fear among Communist China's neighbors if not actually a lessening of tension."[40]

As China strove towards balanced relations with most of its neighbors, relations with Russia continued to sour over a range of issues, including Russia's meddling in China's domestic affairs, Moscow's refusal to go all out in aiding China's military modernization and ideological leadership. Already in 1956, China criticized the Kremlin for its heavy-handed crackdown in Hungary. In 1958, Mao became more eager to stress that China would follow a different path and to criticize the unbalanced relationship. "You think Russians are superior and the Chinese inferior, careless people," Mao threw at the Russian Ambassador. "You want joint ownership, you want everything as joint ownership: our army, our navy, air force, industry, agriculture, culture, education. How about it?" The breaking point came when China refused to accept Moscow's new approach of peaceful competition. The point of departure was that nuclear weapons would render traditional wars useless and that communist countries now had to work towards a zone of peace with the non-aligned countries. For Beijing, such an approach was once more an attempt of the atomic powers to use nuclear deterrence to impose unequal peace. As Khrushchev noted in 1957: "Everybody except Mao was thinking about how to avoid war. We had as slogan 'on with the struggle for peace', yet, suddenly here came Mao Zedong saying we should not be afraid of war." It was Lin Biao who summarized the dilemma most clearly. "The Khrushchev Revisionists claim that if their general line of peaceful coexistence, peaceful transition and peaceful competition is followed, the oppressed will be liberated and a world without weapons and armed forces and without wars will come into existence," he stated. "But the inexorable fact is that imperialism and reaction, headed by the United States, are zealously priming their war machine and are daily engaged in the sanguinary suppression of the revolutionary people and in the threat and use of armed force against independent countries. The kind of rubbish peddled by the Khrushchev revisionists has already taken a great toll of lives in a number of countries." The partnership collapsed when Nikita Khrushchev visited Beijing in 1959. He was parked in a mosquito-infested bungalow in the hills outside the center – undoubtedly retribution for Mao's own frosty stay in a Russian dacha. In 1960, Moscow terminated its economic support. China was on its own.

Exporting Revolution

Meanwhile, China's domestic reforms were in tatters. Agricultural production was largely neglected in the Five-Year Plan. The more factories paced ahead and cities expanded, the less the countryside could follow. The fixation with industrial growth meant that China had to pay enormous prices for purchasing foreign machinery, a price that could only be afforded by putting a heavy fiscal burden on the poor peasants. In 1955, the National People's Congress approved a plan to organize farmers gradually into cooperatives to ramp up agricultural production. Less than a day after the decision, however, Mao personally decided that the cooperatives had to be up and running in less than two years. That decision ended in failure: farming output remained insufficient and the government also became overburdened by the large infrastructure expenses. Cracks in the Party emerged, but Mao pushed through with the Second Five-Year Plan. During the Great Leap Forward, the government kept a timetable that showed how long it would take to catch up with the industrial production of the United Kingdom and the United States. The greater the failure, the more that date was moved up – to 20 years, to 15 years, to seven years, to two years, until the point that Zhou Enlai pragmatically stated that it would happen "within a not so very long historical period." The Great Leap remains one of the darkest pages of China's recent history, costing between 20 and 42 million lives. Between 1960 and 1969, China's gross domestic product did not grow at all, mostly because the losses in agriculture erased the gains in the industrial sector.

This episode coincided with a deterioration in China's international relations. It did sign new agreements with countries like Burma, Sri Lanka, Pakistan, and Afghanistan. By the early 1960s it had also settled its border disputes with Nepal, Burma, North Vietnam, and Outer Mongolia. But China was accused by several neighbors of dumping cheap industrial products and manipulating its expatriate communities. In 1960, Beijing quarreled with the Indonesian government over the latter's mistreatment of Chinese migrants and announced that it would repatriate 600,000 compatriots from Southeast Asia. Tensions over Vietnam grew rapidly. China criticized almost all countries in the region for selling their sovereignty out to the imperialists, while it received the establishment of the Southeast Asian Community, after all an initiative against the great power competition, with a lot of reservations.[41] When the Cultural Revolution broke out in 1966, it elicited scorn in Myanmar, Cambodia, Indonesia, Nepal, and Sri Lanka. Diplomatic relations were broken off with several countries.

Relations with India also went downhill fast. In 1959, Premier Jawaharlal Nehru started to accuse China of sending troops into Ladakh, the western section of the disputed border, and ordered Soviet military gear to clench a fist against China's nibbling strategy. In 1962, the border dispute escalated into a brief war, during which China invaded Indian territory, but then rapidly withdrew, stating that Delhi had learned its lesson. In 1965, China again gathered troops along the border with India, this time to support Pakistan in a clash with India over Kashmir. Japan stood out somewhat as an exception. In 1958, Beijing seized on a small incident – a Japanese student tore down a Chinese flag at a stamp exhibition in Nagasaki – to impose a boycott on the pro-West administration of Premier Kishi. Soon after the setback of 1958, Japan sent a former prime minister to mend fences and both sides agreed to resume trade cooperation a year later. By 1964, after the election of Eisaku Satō as president, relations cooled and Beijing instructed its diplomats to delay trade talks.[42] Throughout the remainder of the 1960s, however, Sino–Japanese relations proved remarkably resilient, which was marked by the opening of a Japanese office in Beijing in 1966, the start of scientific cooperation, and talks of an airline. Tokyo showed a great deal of pragmatism, even during the Cultural Revolution. By 1967, China had become the largest customer of Japanese industrial goods. That year, the two sides renewed their trade pact, even if Japan publicly refused to accept its three principles, which implied Japan severing its relations with Taiwan and the United States. Illustrating the Chinese interest in developing closer relations with Japan, Zhou told a visiting delegation in 1964: "China has basically all the raw materials needed by Japan. Japan can provide China with many varieties of technology and equipment...Both have large markets. As both markets increase in economic stretch, their needs will increase. Thus the opportunities of providing what the other needs will become even greater."

As India moved closer to Russia, China got more estranged from its ally. By the end of the 1960s, the security environment was changing dramatically. The Soviets had started to deploy troops on the border with China, to expand air force bases, and to increase the presence of tactical nuclear missiles.[43] Russian tanks and anti-aircraft units were stationed in Mongolia. Meanwhile, Moscow was cajoling Japan, blaming China for supporting the White Flag Communists in Burma, started normalizing relations with the newly established Suharto Regime in Indonesia, further developed its cooperation with India, and tried to drive a wedge between China and North Vietnam. The brief border skirmishes in 1969, along the Ussuri River in the east and along the border with Xinjiang in the west, marked a historical low in Sino–Soviet relations. With regard to the United States, China clearly tried to avoid a new military confrontation, but that did not prevent Beijing from ordering a new shelling campaign against the island of Quemoy, which allowed China to show its resolve both to the United States and to its own people, and to unleash a propaganda offensive against Washington's interference in South Vietnam and Thailand.[44] In 1961, foreign minister Chen Yi warned that China would respond militarily if the United States, followed by SEATO, would also move into Laos to combat the Soviet-backed rebel groups there. The start of the

Vietnam War in 1965 would further complicate relations. China bristled at peace talks in 1967: "The very aim of the peace talks plot hatched by the United States is to bring about negotiations by cajolery so as to consolidate its position in South Vietnam," Zhou Enlai posited. "As long as the United States does not withdraw its troops, it can carry on endless talks with you so that they may hang there indefinitely."[45]

But the United States started to hint at a rapprochement. Already during the last years of Lyndon Johnson's presidency, Washington made overtures and called on Beijing to avoid isolation.[46] An important signal, the White House authorized payment of its phone bill: US$600,000 in arrears to China's telecommunication department. Soon after the elections of 1969, Richard Nixon's administration hinted at the possibility of lifting trade embargoes and started working toward reducing America's engagement in Vietnam. That made the Thai Prime Minister plead for a more independent foreign policy and President Marcos of the Philippines state that his country had to learn to live with China if America pulled out. The Burmese government also started to tone down its criticism of China and accepted a small batch of earthquake relief aid from China via the Burmese Red Cross. The scene thus seemed ready for a major shift in China's foreign policy.

It was indeed so: Zhou Enlai started to receive foreign delegations and the ministry of foreign affairs reopened its embassies. Yet, at this turning point in Asian power politics, domestic power politics had a decisive impact on China's response. At the time that Washington announced its shift in Southeast Asia, China was still demobilizing its revolutionary red brigades. At the time that tensions with Moscow reached a climax, the pro-Moscow group of generals around Lin Biao started making huge advances in the Chinese leadership, at the expense of the moderates around Zhou Enlai and at the expense of the influence of Mao himself. As John W. Garver reconstructs meticulously, it was this internal power shift that made Beijing cling to the Soviets, even if Mao had indicated already in 1970 that China would like to swap the Soviets for America. Two events were grist to the mill of the pro-Soviet camp. In November 1969, the United States signed a communiqué with Japan that identified Okinawa, South Korea, and Taiwan as essential to Japan's security. In April 1970, American soldiers started pursuing units of the People's Army of Vietnam in eastern Cambodia. This led China to postpone its regular ambassadorial talks in Warsaw. Only after Lin Biao was purged for an alleged coup plot and his plane crashed into the Mongolian plains were Zhou and Mao able to respond to Washington's overtures and to seize the diplomatic opportunities that had slowly become manifest through the turmoil of the revolution.

Revolution and Revisionism

Was China giving up its hopes for an American rapprochement? Not at all. What changed in the first place was not so much China's behavior as its environment. It is true that Zhou Enlai had already steered diplomacy in the direction of pragmatism in the 1950s, but that was overruled by the revolution and internal opposition. It was the prospect of a breakthrough with the United States that changed the security outlook drastically. That was also the case with the pragmatic response of Tokyo to the Cultural Revolution, gradually expanding trade relations, and the more relaxed attitude of some Southeast Asian countries. This proved an important window of opportunity for the moderate politicians in Beijing and for Mao personally, who could only have concluded, especially as his own health deteriorated, that revolutionary zeal would bring China down. The consequences of the nascent diplomatic turnaround, as we will see in the next chapters, would be dramatic, but there would be no changes in China's most important objectives of nation building. Flexible policies, unwavering aspirations! These objectives, it became clear, were through and through revisionist. They required China to curtail the maneuverability of the superpowers and, in the long run, to maximize its power to the point that it would tower above all other Asian countries. That revisionism had nothing to do with evil intentions or an authoritarian scheme for world dominance, as some Congressmen in Washington insisted. China's revisionism, its desire to change the structure of the Asian order and to place itself at the top, was the outcome of justifiable interests. The interesting evolution of the 1960s was that China became more revisionist in its appearance when it became less revisionist in its achievements, that is, the accumulation of power. Revolutionary diplomacy was the nadir of China's revisionism, and not its zenith.

– 3 –

The Normalization

"It takes time for a monkey to become human," Mao Zedong replied when Zhou Enlai came to brief him about his first round of negotiations with Henry Kissinger in July 1971. The National Security Advisor had arrived in Beijing when Lin Biao and his followers were still remonstrating against the rapprochement with the United States. But Mao deemed Kissinger's reassurances sufficient. The bargain was clear. If China would not complicate America's withdrawal from the Vietnam War, this so-called Vietnamization would be followed by gradual reductions in America's military presence in Southeast Asia, South Korea, and Taiwan. Besides that, Kissinger also signaled that his government would not support the Taiwanese Nationalists to attack the mainland or to proclaim independence, recognize China as one of the five major powers, and endorse the five principles of peaceful coexistence.[1] From this moment, the diplomatic change of course became clearer and clearer. In October of that year, Kissinger visited China once more. The same month, a tense marathon meeting of the General Assembly of the United Nations voted overwhelmingly in favor of admitting communist China and expelling the nationalist government. In

November, the program was set for the visit of President Nixon to China. In December, Beijing hardly responded to a five-day American bombing campaign in North Vietnam. In February 1972, finally, President Nixon signed the Shanghai Communiqué that sketched out the principles of Sino–American cooperation. Yet, this winding overture would again be disturbed. In 1976, both Zhou Enlai and Mao Zedong passed away. The radical Gang of Four seized power and purged Deng Xiaoping. It was not until December 1978, at the Third Plenary Session of the Eleventh Central Committee, that the revolutionary debut of modern Chinese politics came to an end, and so, the détente between China, the United States, and most of the rest of the world could be consolidated.

The Détente

Reactions to this détente varied, but were generally positive. After the Shanghai Communiqué, the Soviet Union continued to cajole China with offers to improve relations, while it also strengthened its military presence in Asia, proposed regional security cooperation, and moved closer to India. The Singaporean Minister of Foreign Affairs Sinnathamby Rajaratnam spoke of the most fundamental change in Asian political realities since 1945. Singapore was, together with countries like Japan, Thailand, Malaysia, Laos, and Australia, eager to reach out to China. India, Indonesia, South Korea, the Philippines, and Cambodia were more worried about the strategic repercussions. Adam Malik, Indonesia's Foreign Minister, stated that the time had come for Asian countries to chart more independent international relations: "We must rely on ourselves to develop our country." Likewise, President Ferdinand Marcos announced that the Philippines would respond by pursuing a policy of multiple alignments. The Asian and Pacific Council (ASPAC), an anti-communist organization that included Japan, Australia, New Zealand, the

Philippines, South Korea, South Vietnam, Malaysia, and Taiwan, called for more open membership and would peter away soon afterwards as a consequence of its internal differences on China.[2] Trade helped restore relations with neighboring countries. Many of these relations were re-established by channeling trade through Hong Kong.[3] Japan rose once again to prominence as China's main economic partner in Asia. An important gesture, Japan granted Chinese trade offices diplomatic status in 1972. The support of Japan was reckoned to be crucial in implementing Zhou Enlai's Four Modernizations, officially presented at the National People's Congress in 1975. These modernizations focused on agriculture, industry, national defense, and technology. In February 1978, a long-term trade agreement was signed, providing for the expansion of bilateral trade to US$20 billion by 1985. Japan was expected to export technology, construction materials and machine parts, in return for coal and crude oil.[4]

Meanwhile, China sought to come to grips with explosive disputes, such as the territorial conflict in the East China Sea. The control over that sea returned to the top of the political agenda in 1972, when the United States ceased civil administration over the Ryukyu Islands and returned control of the Senkaku or Diaoyu Islands to Japan. These islands had long been considered Japan's physical markers against influence from the continent – whether imperial or communist. China refused to accept Japanese control over them and advanced its own claim. "We warn the Japanese militarists outright that the Chinese people will never permit the Japanese gangsters to trample on our sacred territory again," a newspaper cried.[5] Tensions built up in 1978, when China sent 100 fishing boats to the area and a Japanese right-wing group erected a lighthouse on one of the islands. Yet, the internal political balances in Japan had come to tilt toward rapprochement, prodded by a new deterioration in relations between the United States and Russia in 1977.[6] Deng Xiaoping cultivated Japan's interest by stating his readiness to drop an anti-Japanese clause from the 1950 alliance treaty with the Soviets. In 1978, a friendship treaty was signed, followed by a statement from Deng that the territorial disputes did not have to spoil relations. "It does not matter if this question is shelved for some time, say ten years. Our generation is not wise enough to find a common language on this question. Our next generation will certainly be wiser." Negotiations about the sea border collapsed a few years after that gentlemen's arrangement. China briefly displayed its frustration by starting exploration activities in 1980, but halted those a short time later. Deputy Premier Yao Yilin called for joint oil development around the Senkaku Islands. Until the early 1990s, the waters separating China and Japan were to remain relatively calm.

Things were different in the South China Sea. Already in 1949, Zhou Enlai had proclaimed the area to be Chinese, putting forward the infamous map with the nine-dashed line.[7] The Premier confirmed this, in 1951, when Japan renounced its claims over the South China Sea Islands in its peace treaty with the allied powers. In 1956, when the French left Indochina, Chinese troops landed in the eastern part of the Paracel or Xisha Islands. In 1958, Chinese fishermen tried to settle on the western part of the Paracel Islands and the government stated that the 12-mile zone that delimits the territorial waters applied to the islands in the South China Sea. The situation became only tenser in the 1970s, with all claimants increasing their presence on the islands, islets and their surrounding waters. In 1971, American reconnaissance planes discovered Chinese convoys with building materials heading for the Paracel Islands.[8] In 1974, just after American troops evacuated from Vietnam, Chinese troops landed on the Paracel Islands, leading to armed clashes with South Vietnamese troops. In the meantime, China stood its ground in international conferences about the Law of the Sea, conferences that provoked many countries to assert their maritime claims. Chinese archaeologists had also started searching around the islands for ancient relics. They recovered porcelain, copper coins, and stone tablets – reportedly as old as the Tang Dynasty. "These finds show once again irrevocably that the Paracel Islands have been Chinese territory since ancient times."[9] In talks with Le Duan, Vietnam's strongman, Vice-Premier Deng Xiaoping reiterated that both the Paracels and the Spratlys were Chinese, but hinted at negotiations. "This problem will naturally form the subject of discussions in the future."[10]

The situation took another turn. Deng was sidelined for two years and hardliners poured vitriol through Chinese newspapers: "The Spratly Islands are part of the sacred territory of China!" More importantly, the reunification of Vietnam, after the fall of Saigon in 1975, prompted Hanoi to search for more Soviet support. Moscow quickly solicited access to Cam Ranh Bay as a hub for its expanding Pacific fleet. As tensions built, a Russian task force, led by the formidable cruiser Admiral Senyavin, was dispatched to the South China Sea.[11] Peking accused Hanoi of becoming the forward post in the Soviet Union's plans to penetrate the Indian Ocean and the Pacific. After the Vietnamese punitive expedition into Cambodia, Beijing ordered its own strike "to teach Vietnam a lesson." In February 1979, hundreds of thousands of troops entered Vietnam. They closed in quickly on Hanoi, but they were supported by only a few hundred tanks and almost no air support. In spite of that, Hanoi came within reach and – this was key – the Soviets did not retaliate. The war was over in March, when China withdrew and started negotiations. These talks in 1979 and 1980 did not lead to a breakthrough, but de-escalated the situation and paved the way for a gradual normalization in the mid-1980s. Meanwhile, China had already signaled that it was interested in handling the conflicts in the South China Sea through diplomatic negotiations when Deputy Premier Li Xiannian accepted an invitation to visit the Philippines in 1978. Throughout most of the 1980s, all claimants tried to increase their presence, by erecting installations on disputed islands, sending more patrol boats into contested waters, and encouraging the exploitation of natural resources like oil and fish. This was destined to lead to incidents and that happened in 1988. What started as a game of surveying and shadowing around Johnson South Reef led to interceptions, soldiers trading shots, and, ultimately, naval artillery firing. About 70 Vietnamese died. China seized six more reefs, but then, once again, started to de-escalate by proposing to shelve the sovereignty issue and to consider joint exploitation of the resources in the South China Sea – very much in the spirit of the gentlemen's agreement with Japan. Deng Xiaoping conveyed to a Vietnamese delegation: "One alternative is to take all these islands back by force; another is to set aside the question and develop them jointly."

Relations with India also moved toward normalization. In 1971, during the Bangladesh Liberation War, Chinese troops exerted pressure on the Indian border. In 1975, for reasons still unknown, Chinese soldiers killed four Indian border guards in Arunachal Pradesh.[12] The incident did not escalate. Premier Indira Gandhi had to spend all her efforts on domestic rivals. During the state of emergency, Indian armed forces were deployed to repress protests instead of securing the border. Delhi also sought to reduce its dependence on the Soviet Union. In 1976, India proposed to exchange ambassadors, for the first time since the border war of 1962. In 1978, a Chinese economic delegation toured India for three weeks, followed by a visit by Wang Pingnan, which paved the way for border negotiations. That year, the new Prime Minister Morarji Desai paid a visit to Washington during which he underscored the importance of a closer relationship. Simultaneously, New Delhi revived negotiations with Pakistan. This evolution broadened the scope for interaction significantly. In 1979, China invited Foreign Minister Vajpayee to discuss bilateral political and economic relations. Desai's scope to respond positively was severely constrained. Opposition, including Indira Gandhi, blamed him for soft-soaping China and being a weak statesman. Nevertheless, he resisted calls for more assertiveness. A quarrel over Tibetan herdsmen in Bhutan, the so-called Yak War, did not affect the rapprochement. In 1981, the first round of border talks took place, without results, but with a promise from Foreign Minister Huang Hua that China would support cooperation in science and trade regardless of the territorial impasse.

Marble Floor Guerrilla

Whether it concerned Japan, Vietnam, or India, China increasingly resorted to legal ambiguity and economic cooperation to defuse territorial tensions. In that regard, the 1970s were an important turning point. What changed, however, was not China's effort to maximize its power. That remained the most important objective. What changed was China's security environment and the choice for more effective policies. From its inferior position, China would pursue the same guerrilla fight but this time on the marble floors of international gatherings and trade fairs. After the Gang of Four was neutralized, it was realized quickly what was *not* an effective way to build a coherent and strong nation: instability largely caused by personal cult, the self-defeating pursuit of autarchy, and international isolation. What really made this period a turning point was that several domestic experiments with economic reform – especially those by Zhao Zhiyang in the Province of Sichuan – proved fruitful and promising enough to be gradually turned into an alternative to the economic collectivism of the previous decades. The success of the newly industrialized economies attracted the attention of Chinese leaders as well. The craving of the Chinese people to escape hardship and this flicker of hope for an alternative created new momentum. That momentum could only be sustained thanks to Beijing's more positive international environment. In many ways, the major powers continued to change their attitude, not China. The adjustments of the major powers were followed by changes in the behavior of the smaller countries. Australia's Ambassador to China, Stephen FitzGerald, summarized this as follows: "The current Chinese attempt to break out from political quarantine and re-order its relationships with non-recognizing countries echoes a policy which has been tried with varying degrees of publicity and enthusiasm since 1954. The difference is that, on this occasion, these countries are willing not only to talk but to take the initiative."[13]

Nothing of that affected China's revisionist agenda and the four great aspirations. During Deng's leadership, China reiterated the objective of creating a new international order. That still implied a global redistribution of economic power and that China needed to catch up with the developed countries. During the path-breaking Third Plenary Session of the Eleventh Central Committee in 1978, for example, the objective was restated to "advance in the new long march to make China a modern, powerful socialist country before the end of this century" and "to catch up with America and to surpass Britain," which would effectively imply surpassing all the neighboring countries. In 1981, Deng Xiaoping reiterated the goal to quadruple China's GDP by 2001 and to reach high-income status by the middle of the twenty-first century.[14] The strategic repercussions of this economic transition were clear. First of all, it meant that China would become a strong and independent economic player. Whatever role foreign companies were to play in the first decades of the great opening up, the long-term objective was to reduce China's dependence on those players and to control the most important economic assets itself.[15] As Deng put it: "At the present stage, a developing country that wants to develop its national economy must first of all keep its natural resources in its own hands and gradually shake off the control of foreign capital." As regards technological development, Deng remarked: "We must rely on our own efforts, develop our own creativity and persist in the policy of independence and self-reliance.

But independence does not mean shutting the door on the world."

Equally important were the political repercussions that China anticipated. From the mid-1980s, for example, China was more and more convinced that it could become a key player in an emerging multipolar order. At the beginning, this was mostly a matter of China playing the leader of the third world. In 1981, for instance, Zhang Mingyang, the Director of the World Institute of International Problems, wrote that increasing unity among the developing countries was the driving force behind the multipolarization of the global order.[16] This, he continued, led both to a diversification of values and interests and to a reduction of the influence of the superpowers. Gradually, however, it became clear that China expected an autonomous role as one of the major powers. In an interview with the *Far Eastern Economic Review* in 1981, Foreign Minister Wu Xueqian argued that the trend towards multipolarity would lead states to act more independently to protect their interests.[17] If Deng Xiaoping in 1985 still brushed off the idea of "a big power triangle" composed of the Soviet Union, the United States and China, he insisted five years later that China did not have to belittle its own importance. "If the world becomes three-polar, four-polar or five-polar ... China too will be a pole."[18] This linkage between economic power and international influence became very important. Remarked Deng: "The role we play in international affairs is determined by the extent of our economic growth. If our country becomes more developed and prosperous, we will be in a position to play a greater role in international affairs. Already our international role is not insignificant. With a stronger material base, we will be able to enhance it."[19] Chinese leaders also considered it to be essential to return Taiwan and to gain military clout. An important article put it as follows: "Many American leaders believe that as long as the United States opposes Soviet expansionism, China will not care very much about the Taiwan issue. If some people still believe that Sino–American relations can only be based on opposition to other countries' hegemonic acts, then this is a retreat. If they believe that China will agree to this retreat, then this is a dream."[20]

The development of a strong economy would inevitably lead to a strong military. The upgrading of China's military power was even included as one of the Four Modernizations. "We must strive to gain more time to improve our military equipment and educate and train our army well so as to reduce unnecessary losses. If we can gain a relatively long time free of war, that will enable us to continue modernizing the army, raising its combat effectiveness and making our preparations for defense," explained Deng Xiaoping. Yet, economics came first. Deng insisted that the first three modernizations were the most urgent and that the military would get its share when those three had been achieved.[21] In 1981, military spending was cut from 21 billion yuan to 17 billion yuan.[22] In 1985, 1 million troops were transferred to the civilian sector, another 500,000 ten years later. More money was put aside to prepare the military for war under modern conditions, the new guideline for military campaigns. This especially benefited programs for nuclear weapons, aircraft, submarines, communication, missiles, and weapons for land forces. During the 1980s, however, China struggled to build competitive defense industries and more development programs were transferred to civilian industries.

The prospect of China becoming a major power and the leading power in Asia was a unsettling one, and the Chinese knew it. Chinese leaders were keen to stress that their country would not seek hegemony, would refrain from aggression and that it would always be part of the third world. Such statements, however, were not matched by changes in China's strategic calculations. It is true that China came to see armed conflict as less likely. If before 1978 the Party line was that war remained inevitable, this changed in the following years. As tensions with the Soviets abated, Chinese leaders contemplated that a peaceful rise would be possible – at least for a while. Throughout official statements, it becomes clear that China still expected its growth to clash with the interests of other countries. When Deng Xiaoping met with President Jimmy Carter, he spoke of *postponing* a major war: "To realize our Four Modernizations, we need a prolonged period of a peaceful environment. But even now we believe the Soviet Union will launch a war. But if we act well and properly, it is possible to postpone it. China hopes to postpone a war for twenty-two years." This was echoed in an important editorial that called for the Chinese to do the utmost to postpone war so as to gain time in China's favor.[23]

With Japan it spoke of shelving the East China Sea dispute, not of solving it. Likewise, it proposed that India pursue cooperation, and leave the border dispute for future negotiations. In regard to Taiwan, Beijing made an effort to mollify it, but leaders like Hu Yaobang also made clear that China did not rule out the use of military force and even suggested that time was needed to convince Taiwan of China's strength. In 1985, the Central Military Commission stated: "It is a possibility that war on a large scale will not break out for a relatively long period of time." This all seems to fit with the 24-character dictum that emerged in the early 1990s.[24] "Observe calmly. Secure our position. Cope with affairs calmly. Hide our capacities and bide our time. Be good at maintaining a low profile. Never claim leadership." At the same time, there is ample evidence that Chinese observers expected to get the upper hand over the other Asian powers.[25] Reforms in India were going nowhere.[26] Southeast Asian growth remained fragile.[27] The Soviets were in difficulties. The Japanese miracle started to lose its luster.[28] Deng Xiaoping also encouraged the province of Guangdong to get on a par with the Four Little Dragons – South Korea, Taiwan, Singapore and Hong Kong. In 1975, Mao Zedong had backed a plan to develop an ocean-going navy. In 1987, the celebrated naval strategist Liu Huaqing revealed a plan to alter the military balance to China's advantage, first beyond Taiwan by 2000, beyond Japan and the Philippines by 2025, and as far as Hawaii by 2050.

Opening Up

The 1980s were the period during which the great opening up was consolidated. Whereas the Chinese government continued to adhere to principles of economic sovereignty and self-strengthening, the way was cleared for foreign businesses to start operating in the People's Republic. In 1980, the National People's Congress passed regulations for establishing a special economic zone in Guangdong and Shenzhen. To streamline its foreign trade policies, four different ministries and commissions were integrated into the newly created Ministry of Foreign Economic Relations and Trade (MOFERT). At the same time, provinces received more authority to build their own foreign trade corporations and to expand economic relations abroad. Asia was clearly at the core of China's economic opening-up policies. During the 1980s, economic relations were normalized with most Asian countries. Trade offices were established in 12 different countries.

In Southeast Asia, Thailand became one of the main diplomatic successes. Thai companies were among the first to start investing in China and Chinese companies were allowed to enter Thailand's market for construction projects and labor service cooperation. Singapore and the Philippines became the other two main trade partners in Southeast Asia. Progress in Malaysia was slower, but during a visit to Beijing in 1985, Malaysia's Prime Minister Mohamad Mahathir declared that: "while politics dominated the first decade of Sino–Malaysian relations, economics should dominate the next decade." Because of domestic opposition, it was only in 1988 that the first economic agreements were signed. Likewise, the Indonesian Foreign Minister Mochtar announced in 1984 that his country wished to resume direct trade with China.[29] While direct trade had nominally started, Indonesia refused to let the PRC establish a trade office, which the military was afraid the PRC might use to carry out subversive activities. In 1986, representatives of the two countries negotiated an agreement via Singapore. China approached these Southeast Asian countries by presenting its growing market as an opportunity for increasing exports, especially in the agricultural sector. It also continued to offer oil at friendship prices to states like Thailand, the Philippines and Singapore. In 1988, border trade resumed with archenemy Vietnam and both sides started rebuilding the grassy border roads that had been destroyed during the long episode of conflict.[30]

Trade relations with Japan and South Korea expanded further. China's leaders became anxious that the surge in Japanese investment abroad and the relocation of sections of Japanese industry in East Asia could pass by China and favor Taiwan. "We should appreciate it if all enterprises in your country strengthened their cooperation with us. We hope the Japanese government will encourage them to take a longer-range view. China is short of funds, so that it has been unable to develop many of its resources," Deng Xiaoping informed Premier Yasuhiro Nakasone during a visit to Tokyo in 1984. "If they are developed, we shall be able to supply more of Japan's needs. And if Japan invests in China now, it will benefit greatly in future." Expanding ties with South Korea and Japan in turn prompted Taiwanese businesses to press for a faster relaxation of restrictions on Taiwanese investment in China. While Taipei did not relinquish its "three no's" policy – no direct exchanges by mail, trade, or air and shipping services – many of the barriers to direct trade, investment, and visits were lowered. During this period, Hong Kong consolidated its position as commercial interface. By the mid-1980s, about 80 percent of the foreign investors in China operated from Hong Kong. More than three million citizens in the Province of Guangdong worked for Hong Kong manufacturers.

Trade also helped smooth relations with the Soviet Union. In 1984, Beijing and Moscow signed an agreement on economic and technical cooperation and established a commission to oversee its implementation. In 1985, they agreed to build seven new industrial enterprises in China. As a consequence of this reciprocal policy of mild overtures, trade between the Russian Far East and border provinces like Heilongjiang and Xinjiang expanded dramatically.[31] Moscow led the restoration of friendly relations. In 1985, the anti-Chinese leader in Mongolia was replaced. In 1986, Mikhail Gorbachev gave an important speech in Vladivostok in which he vowed to reduce troops along the border, to position no additional missiles in the east, and to consider withdrawal from Mongolia. China balked. It also wanted Russia to stop supporting Vietnam. In 1987, border negotiations started. In 1989, with the Soviet Union already groaning towards its collapse, Moscow acquiesced in Chinese control over the Spratly Islands. It also pressured Vietnam to back down on Cambodia and withdrew its navy from Cam Ranh Bay. In May of that year, President Gorbachev paid his humbling visit to Beijing. The Soviet threat was gone. During its slow retreat, trade had grown ten-fold.

The demise of the Soviet Union encouraged several other countries to pursue normalization with China. In 1985, Laos made a first attempt, but China did not respond, until 1989. In 1988, Vietnam discretely approached China to restore relations, but China balked, until January 1989, when Hanoi started withdrawing its troops from Cambodia. In spite of its domestic criticism, the Indian government too continued to work toward closer relations. Trade proved once again an important facilitator. "We cannot afford not to understand each other," Deng explained to a visiting Indian delegation in 1982. "If we want to change the international economic order, we must, above all, settle the question of relations between the South and the North, but at the same time we have to find ways to increase South–South cooperation." Two years later, a first trade agreement was concluded. After six rounds of border negotiations, relations broke off briefly when the Indian Parliament announced the creation of Arunachal Pradesh as a Union State in December 1986. This démarche enraged the Chinese government. Deng Xiaoping warned India not to take possession of disputed terrain. During the months following the act, troops mobilized on both sides of the border and media reports even mentioned new skirmishes. However, this time violence did not escalate and both countries backed away after the Indian and Chinese Ministers of Foreign Affairs met in New York. Tensions built up further in 1978, during the so-called Sumdorong Chu conflict, which led to alarming military deployments along the border and both governments warning that they would not back down. China was particularly worried that India would send more troops into disputed areas, like Tawang and Demchok. In May 1987, however, the Indian External Affairs Minister was sent to Beijing to bring an end to this brief episode of unrest. In 1988 Rajiv Gandhi paid a historic visit to China, despite opposition from the media and several Congress Party members. During this visit he had lengthy conversations with Deng Xiaoping. "The world is changing, so people's minds have to change with it," Deng said. From then onwards cooperation would gather pace, exchanges proliferate, and business boom, but the border dispute remained unsolved.

China also started to recognize the importance of multilateral organizations. In 1980, it reclaimed its place on the United Nations Interim Commission for the International Trade Organization, in 1983 it joined the Multi-Fiber Arrangement and in 1986 it "re-entered" the General Agreement on Tariffs and Trade (GATT).[32] These memberships were helpful in expanding export revenues, needed for financing the government's modernization plans. Second, they added to China's image as a rising power that was largely cooperative toward other protagonists. Third, Beijing was seeking to outmaneuver Taiwan. The same mixture of political and economic interests prompted

Beijing not to remain absent from regional organizations
in Asia. In 1986, it regained its position in the Asian Development Bank (ADB) as the sole legal representative of
China, while Taiwan was allowed to remain with the
altered designation of Taipei, China.[33] In 1988, it joined
the Pacific Economic Cooperation Conference (PECC), a
non-governmental forum established at the initiative of
Australia.[34] If it still resisted ASEAN's role in brokering a
Kampuchea settlement in 1981, China announced in 1984
that it wished to establish "a long-term, stable, good-
neighborly, and friendly relationship" with the regional
grouping. In 1985, China was invited by Indonesia to
attend a first ASEAN business conference.[35] During his
visit to Thailand in 1988, Premier Li Peng urged the establishment of economic relations with ASEAN. The same
year, Beijing started negotiating membership of the Pacific
Basin Economic Council (PBEC), a semi-official forum
supported by Japan and Australia. While being held up by
the fallout from the Tiananmen crisis, China also showed
itself eager to join the Asia-Pacific Economic Cooperation
forum (APEC). In 1989, talks started with Beijing to find
a formula for including both mainland China and Taiwan.
The Chinese government agreed to membership of Taiwan
and Hong Kong as economic entities, and in 1990 the
green light was given for China to enter.

Another important element in China's evolving regional
trade policy was the role of provinces in establishing ties
with neighboring countries. The constitution of 1982 gave
these sub-state entities more leeway in pursuing their own
economic diplomacy. They were, for example, allowed to
set up Overseas Chinese Affairs Offices and Foreign Economic and Trade Commissions. Many of them started
organizing trade fairs, economic missions abroad, and
their own presence in Chinese embassies. Coastal provinces invested massively in their ties with Japan, Taiwan,
and Hong Kong. In the 1980s, Jilin started championing
regional economic cooperation around the Tumen River,
which it saw as a chance to become a trade hub between

China and neighboring countries like Russia and South Korea. In 1985, Yunnan made temporary provisions on border trade and a few years later, the governor visited Burma, opening department stores and marketing Chinese goods.[36] As soon as trade was restored with Vietnam in 1988, Guangxi Province pushed for an early settlement of the border dispute, a flexible customs regime, and refurbishment of the transport infrastructure to border cities.

Steady Course

The economic reforms and charm offensive proved most effective. China outpaced most of its neighbors and probably also diverted economic opportunities away from them. In 1978, foreign direct investments in China were almost negligible, but they reached US$3 billion in 1989 and from then onwards continued to grow spectacularly. At the same time, foreign direct investment inflows stagnated or even decreased in several other Asian countries. In India, for instance, investment inflows dropped for five consecutive years after 1987, in the Philippines the five years after 1988, and in Thailand the five years after 1990.[37] In merchandise exports, the trend was not yet that pronounced. China's share of the region's exports grew slightly from 9 percent in 1978 to 12 percent in 1988. But by 1988, it had dwarfed India and clearly started to outpace Southeast Asia, whose export growth rate shrank from 25 percent in 1988 to 12 percent in 1992. China's project of nation building had finally touched firm economic ground and that was the most important achievement under Deng Xiaoping's leadership. Besides that, China's neighborhood policy also changed remarkably: it became more professional, more diverse, more multilateral, and more flexible. For all that, the new flexibility had its limitations. None of the four great aspirations were revised, no major concessions were made on the goal to recover lost territory, and even if China cooperated more with the superpowers, it did not backtrack from its aspiration to curtail their privileges by changing the global order. To do so, its leaders were convinced they needed to hold a steady course. The Tiananmen crisis of 1989 would not change that.

— 4 —

Briefcase Revisionism

On June 24, 1989, barely 20 days after tanks had driven the last groups of students from Tiananmen Square, a new groan of frustration went through the Chinese capital. It followed the news that an uncharismatic apparatchik from Shanghai had just been appointed as the new Secretary General of the Communist Party. Jiang Zemin was a compromise figure. In Shanghai, it was the energetic mayor Zhu Rongji who was driving the reforms, not him. But the 62-year-old politician scored some points with the hardliners in the Party by running the propaganda offensive against the protest movement. As the new national leader, Jiang was expected to accomplish two important tasks: to regain the confidence of the Chinese people and to limit the diplomatic fallout of the Tiananmen crisis. The second task turned out to be not all that difficult. However loud the cries of indignation in Western societies, the diplomatic responses remained remarkably muted. The American government imposed sanctions, but was careful not to get too carried away by the criticism from Capitol Hill. "Our foreign policy must really keep open the possibility and indeed encourage China's full return to the international community," Secretary of State James Baker said.[1]

In Europe, Belgium and Italy halted their economic aid, but, at the same time, the British Prime Minister Margaret Thatcher warned that hastened sanctions could cause panic in Hong Kong. It was among China's Asian neighbors, however, that governments were most afraid to overreact. "We cannot tolerate the Chinese government's human rights abuse, but also should not push China into a position of isolation from the international community," the Japanese Minister of Foreign Affairs stated.[2] The South Korean government only remarked that the bloodshed at Tiananmen Square was "regrettable". Brunei, in its capacity as the chairman of ASEAN, considered Tiananmen a strictly internal affair. The only exception was the Philippines, which decided to freeze its political relations and, moreover, to stop Chinese imports, albeit that the latter was more an attempt to address its growing trade imbalance. China was thus not as much on the defensive as is often claimed. In fact, in the decade following the Tiananmen crisis, China's neighbors were at least as determined to prevent the giant from slithering back into retrenchment as the new Chinese leadership was to avoid it.

The Turn

Throughout the 1990s, China's neighborhood policy certainly came to look more dynamic. In 1993, Premier Li Peng stressed in his annual report that "the development of beneficial and friendly relations with neighboring states, and the striving for a peaceful and tranquil surrounding environment are important aspects of our country's foreign affairs." In 1997, Jiang Zemin formulated the diplomatic priorities as follows: respect for sovereignty and different political, economic, and cultural cooperation, non-interference, shelving differences and finding common ground for cooperation, the resolution of disagreements through peaceful means, and promoting multipolarity. It led China to invest heavily in regional cooperation, which was praised as an indicator of growing flexibility. In 1991, it joined the Asia-Pacific Economic Cooperation (APEC) and the Tumen River Area Development Programme (TRADP), a United Nations-backed scheme for development in Northeast Asia. That year, China was also invited by Malaysia as a guest to the ministerial meeting of ASEAN. At that time, ASEAN still consisted of only six members; Vietnam, Myanmar, Laos, and Cambodia would join between 1997 and 1999. In 1992, the ASEAN Secretary General proposed the establishment of two joint committees, which China keenly accepted. In 1994, China became a member of the ASEAN Regional Forum, together with the United States, Japan, South Korea, and seven other countries. In 1995, China joined the Greater Mekong Sub-region (GMS), a project through which the Asian Development Bank wanted to promote cooperation in the Mekong River basin. In 1996, it was accepted as a dialogue partner of ASEAN and negotiations were started for membership of the Central Asia Regional Economic Cooperation (CAREC). Moreover, China was the driving force behind the Shanghai Five, a cooperation platform with Kazakhstan, Kyrgyzstan, Russia, Tajikistan, and Uzbekistan. President Jiang Zemin seized the informal China–ASEAN Summit of 1997 to convey to his counterparts the following message: "Give priority to economic relations and trade, scientific and technological cooperation between our two sides in accordance with the principle of drawing on each other's comparative advantages and mutual benefit, and reinforce cooperation in the areas of resources, technology, banking, information, human resources development and investment so as to promote each other for common progress."[3] The year after, ASEAN, China, Japan, and, South Korea established the ASEAN+3 meetings and, by 1999, the first noises emerged of a free trade agreement within the grouping.[4]

This participation in regional organizations brings us to a second change in China's relations with Asia: communication. In 1994, Foreign Minister Qian Qishen proposed to develop more multi-level and multi-channel dialogue mechanisms at both bilateral and regional levels. Since then China has eagerly seized opportunities to broaden communication. The frequency of official bilateral visits was increased almost exponentially, thanks also to the gradual expansion of relevant ministries and the enlargement of Chinese embassies, especially in the late 1990s. "The Chinese clearly came to see bilateral exchanges as a yardstick of progress," a Singaporean diplomat remarked, "but it took them some time also to learn to use these exchanges to make practical progress. Language was often a problem, personal skills too, but definitely also the lack of clear instructions from Beijing."[5] Another official said: "The quantitative leap in our exchanges was not matched by a marked improvement in the quality of our talks. The Chinese leaders became certainly more confident, but for the lower levels of officials, it took at least a decade to go beyond the traditional lecturing and finger pointing."[6] The official gatherings were flanked by many new informal dialogues, the so-called track-2 and track-1.5 meetings. A host of such meetings developed around the partnership with ASEAN, most of them focusing on trade and identifying opportunities for deepening economic cooperation. Other platforms were the Northeast Asia Cooperation Dialogue (NEACD) and the Council for Security and Cooperation in the Asia Pacific (CSCAP). Business-to-business exchanges were another channel in which China invested a lot. During the tenure of Jiang Zemin, joint economic committees were set up with at least nine Asian countries.

The expansion of economic cooperation coincided with a third trend: the proliferation of actors involved in diplomatic affairs. Provinces, for example, took the lead in building synergies with neighboring countries. Xinjiang and Inner Mongolia were the ones behind China's accession to CAREC. Yunnan and Guangxi pushed relentlessly for better access to Southeast Asia. Sichuan province launched the idea of a new Southwest Silk Road to promote exports to Bangladesh and India. By 2000, coastal provinces had teamed up with neighboring countries in subregional initiatives around the Pearl River Delta, the Gulf of Tonkin, the Yellow Sea, and the Bohai Bay.

A fourth change was China's growing propensity to raise expectations as a business partner and as a responsible partner. The share of China in most Asian countries' exports remained small – about 5 percent on average in 1995.[7] But the expectations were high, especially toward China as an investment opportunity for export-oriented manufacturers. Between 1991 and 1995, China attracted US$12 billion of foreign direct investments from Taiwan, US$8 billion from Japan, US$4 billion from Singapore, US$2 billion from South Korea, and US$2 billion from other Southeast Asian countries – more than double by the end of the century.[8] To facilitate these flows, China signed 16 bilateral investment protection agreements with Asian countries. The eagerness for the Chinese market only increased after the Asian Financial Crisis of 1997 and 1998. From that moment, China's economy raced ahead much faster than that of most of its neighbors. China played the crisis cleverly. Thanks to its reserves, it could spend US$1 trillion of emergency investment on new infrastructure. This investment-driven stimulus, small short-term external debt, and capital account controls also allowed China to stay out of a series of competitive devaluations among the Asian countries. The gains were significant. Not only was China able to assert itself as a stable market for investors; its decision not to devalue the yuan against other Asian currencies allowed leaders to trumpet China's solidarity and responsibility. "During the recent financial crisis in Southeast Asia, China has participated within its own capacity in the bailout plan of international financial organizations. China has paid the price and made the sacrifice for the stability of Asia economy by not devaluing its own currency," Minister Long Yongtu stated in 1999. "In spite of the difficulties caused by the Southeast Asia's financial crisis, China, at this session, still decided to honour its commitment." As if that were not enough, it readied to join the World Trade Organization.

Responsibility was also what China tried to show in security affairs. It did so in some of the negotiations about land borders. With Vietnam, Laos, Tajikistan, and Kazakhstan, for example, it made concessions on patches of disputed land. In 1995, it also started to develop a new security concept designed to reassure neighbors and emphasize the difference from American unilateralism. When it was made public, the concept turned out to borrow heavily from the Five Principles of Peaceful Coexistence, stressing sovereignty and equality, but it put new emphasis on informal security dialogue, cooperation on new security threats, the prevention of the proliferation of weapons of mass destruction, building confidence in conflict zones, and the role of regional organizations. The armed forces also became an important tool to create goodwill. By the early 1990s, high-level military exchanges were set up with Russia, India, and, albeit reluctantly, Japan. The Chinese navy made port calls in Thailand, the Philippines, Malaysia, Pakistan, India, Sri Lanka, North Korea, Singapore, Australia, New Zealand, Russia, and the United States. With India, Russia, and the Central Asian countries it agreed to reduce military force throughout the region. In 1999, China also deployed 200 paramilitary troops as part of a United Nations mission in East Timor, after it had backed an Australia-led intervention. All this led a growing number of observers to deduce that China had a penchant for accommodation and the status quo. In his widely read article, Alistair Ian Johnston wrote of China as a committed participant in the existing order. Think-tankers Bates Gill and James Reilly found that China's more flexible stance on sovereignty and intervention paved the way for "greater integration into international society, greater acceptance of international norms, establishing a new multilateral confidence-building measure to gain greater Chinese military transparency while reducing regional distrust of China, and spreading the burden of and strengthening international support for UN peace-keeping."[9] Argued Australian Professor Stuart Harris: "China has moved from an emphasis on political-strategic concerns to a more all-embracing view of national interest, to accept that the international system is not invariably hostile." Morgan Stanley's chief economist, Stephen Roach, who would make China-optimism his trademark, asserted that a new benevolent Asian leader was emerging. Or was it?

Standing Strong

China may have become more forthcoming in its style during that period, but its core objectives, its interests, and even its anarchic worldviews remained unaffected. Nothing demonstrated that more compellingly than its attitude toward the Southeast Asian countries, South Korea, Japan, the Soviet Union, and Taiwan. Consider Vietnam. In 1989, negotiations with Hanoi over its involvement in Cambodia had been going on for almost a year and throughout these talks Beijing refused to make any concession on its core demands: Vietnam had to withdraw its tens of thousands of soldiers before China would cease its support for the armed opponents of President Hun Sen, and the Khmer Rouge had to have a role in Cambodia's political transition. China shrewdly exploited Moscow's desire to normalize relations by demanding that it exert more pressure on Vietnam. It also made use of Vietnam's desperation to get American aid, aid that the Americans too tied to withdrawal from Cambodia. The Chinese had thus only to be patient. Secret negotiations with the Vietnamese Vice Foreign Minister in the spring of 1989 had gone nowhere, until Hanoi declared in April that its soldiers in Cambodia would be gone by the end of the year. In June, China made a few gestures, by expressing its appreciation to the Vietnamese Foreign Minister for Vietnam's restraint in reacting to China's Tiananmen crackdown. In July, the *Shanghai*

Liberation Daily credited Hun Sen with having improved Cambodia's economy. In November, at last, a United Nations resolution was passed that indirectly gave the Khmer Rouge a role in an interim government. It would take another two years for the tensions to abate. Meanwhile, China continued to provide the Khmer Rouge with mortars, anti-aircraft guns, rocket launchers, and heavy artillery. But China got its way: Vietnam was out of Cambodia and, equally important, the Russians were out of Vietnam. Growing frustrations between Beijing and the Khmer Rouge, and an attack by Khmer Rouge combatants on Chinese peacekeepers in Cambodia, would do the rest. In September 1990, Deputy Prime Minister Vu Nguyen Giap arrived in China to attend the Asian Games, the highest-level official visit since 1979. About a year later, Communist Party boss Du Muoi called on Beijing for a summit meeting that formalized the normalization.

The improvement in relations with Cambodia permitted China to advance its relations with the rest of Southeast Asia. Indonesia came first. Already in February 1989, China and Indonesia had agreed to normalize relations, more than two decades after they were suspended over allegations of China supporting a communist coup. Indonesia was running a large trade surplus with China and powerful tycoons had prodded President Suharto to put aside his reservations. Foreign Minister Ali Alatas considered closer ties with China crucial to gaining regional influence vis-à-vis Thailand.[10] In July 1990, diplomatic relations between Beijing and Jakarta were officially restored. Singapore followed three months later. In the wake of Tiananmen, Beijing had dispatched its trade minister to the city-state and refrained from criticism when Singapore offered to host US military facilities.[11] Next came Laos, a close ally of Vietnam.[12] More than half of Laos's foreign investments came from China and these commercial links continued to expand rapidly.[13] In 1991, diplomatic relations were established with Brunei. China had dispatched a first trade delegation to the tiny sultanate in October 1989, and its hosts proved most ready to sell oil. Later on, ties were picked up with the Philippines. Already in 1992, Manila demanded that the United States withdraw from the Subic Bay naval base. In 1993, President Fidel Ramos visited China. Malaysia too hurried to strengthen relations. In 1993, Premier Mohammed Mahathir headed a business delegation of 290 participants to Beijing. Besides business, Mahathir considered China a crucial part of his quest for a more independent foreign policy and the setting up of an East Asia Economic Caucus (EAEC) as an alternative to APEC.

China also commenced to work closer with ASEAN.[14] It is often said that China took the initiative in engaging the regional grouping. Indeed, China was particularly interested in its resources, its technology – and its industries.[15] Even if Chinese experts stressed economic complementarity, it was clear that Beijing wanted the heavy investments from Japan, Taiwan, South Korea, and other developed countries for itself. Moreover, it had an interest in limiting the traditional influence of Japan and resisting the efforts of Tokyo to build more structured and legally binding regional organizations. In 1992, Japan proposed to broaden the agenda of the Japan–ASEAN Forum, which was established back in 1977 by its energetic Prime Minister Fukuda Takeo. But China was pushing against an open door. The ASEAN members were desperate to export to China and its secretariat keen to facilitate closer economic relations. The Southeast Asian countries also saw a partnership between ASEAN and the regional powers as an opportunity to gain leverage. In the same way that Beijing expected to use regional bodies to manage fear, its neighbors hoped to use regional schemes to mold China's ambitions.

Once again, progress was offset by several setbacks. More than in the 1980s even, China became perceived as an assertive juggernaut, sturdily throwing its weight around in the South China Sea. In hindsight, however, this perception was not entirely correct. China was a persistent power, by any measure. It stuck to its claims on all the islands within the nine-dashed line. It stuck to its consequent claim on the territorial waters and the exclusive economic zones around most of these islands. It also continued to insist that exclusive economic zones would be open to civilian ships, but not to military vessels, which was an effort mostly to reduce the freedom of action of the American navy. It was persistent also in showing its resolve, resisting conflicting assertions by other countries, and opposing interference of other powers like the United States. But it did not become much more assertive than countries like Vietnam and the Philippines. All sides pushed their markers.

Consider the development of military facilities. By 1990, China had turned Woody Island, part of the Paracel or Xisha group, into a military stronghold, complete with a long runway, but the Philippines had done the same much earlier on Kalayaan Island, Taiwan on Taiping Island, and Vietnam on Spratly Island, and Malaysia had commenced similar works on Shallow Reef.[16] A report of 1992 stated that some thousand soldiers, sailors, and construction workers were present on 21 islands. By 1999, 46 islands in the Spratly Archipelago were garrisoned: 27 by Vietnam, 8 by the Philippines, and 7 by China. China had dispatched 260 troops, against 600 from Vietnam and 595 from the Philippines.[17] Neither was China the only party that pursued legal unilateralism. The 1975 constitution of Vietnam, for instance, had already asserted its jurisdiction over a large part of the South China Sea. The 1987 constitution of the Philippines went even further and included very concrete clauses on how its parts of the Sea had to be managed. When China issued its Law on the Territorial Sea and the Contiguous Zone in February 1992, it thus came rather late. It was also not the first to use economic activities to affirm its claims. All countries had been supporting the fishing industry. Malaysia, the Philippines, and Indonesia also started promoting tourism on and around disputed islands.[18]

The list of incidents is long. In 1991, Vietnam reported that China had deployed troops on Woody Island. In February 1992 came China's Law on the Territorial Sea and, four months later, China announced a deal with Crestone Corporation for oil exploration in an area that Vietnam had already carved up into blocks for its own future drilling programs. China offered to split production as long as it retained sovereignty. Vietnam declined and invited a Norwegian company to prepare similar exploration. Vietnamese ships repeatedly haunted Chinese oil exploration ships. In July 1992, China occupied the Da Lac reef and reportedly deployed three conventional submarines to patrol the area around the reef. In 1993, China irked Indonesia by revealing a new map that indicated the Natuna Islands as a part of its territory. Beijing later explained that it did not claim Natuna, but that there were overlaps in exclusive economic zones. In 1995, making use of the absence of the Philippine navy during the monsoon season, Chinese troops landed on the Mischief Reef and constructed three structures. This would be followed by a series of confrontations between Chinese fishing boats and naval vessels around the reef, but the Philippines did not make any effort to reclaim the reef.

At the same time, China started to participate in a range of dialogues. Throughout that process, the dialogues gradually took on a more formal character, which China used to broaden the scope for cooperation in the South China Sea. However, it remained stubborn in resisting any territorial concession, participation of external powers, or international arbitration. In 1990, China also participated in a first Indonesian workshop on the South China Sea, but it insisted on limiting this initiative to academics only. In the second session in 1991, China tabled specific proposals for cooperation on navigations channels, the exchange of meteorological data, and sea rescue. In 1992, it proposed joint marine research, and in 1993 the promotion of confidence building, which was picked up as the main focus of the fifth and last workshop in 1995. The main drawback of the meetings was that China saw them as a tool to ease pressure, whereas the others used them to put more pressure on China. In 1992, foreign minister Qian Qichen indicated that China was interested in a multi-level and multi-channel dialogue mechanism on security with ASEAN, but that China also wanted to settle disputes through quiet diplomacy. During Jiang Zemin's historic visit to Hanoi in 1994, both sides agreed to set up a joint working group to discuss the territorial disputes in the Spratly Islands – it would not make any progress. The ASEAN Regional Forum (ARF) would not ease the territorial conundrum either.[19] China did become an active member and sponsored different issues on confidence building, but it refused to use the forum for discussions on the South China Sea. The only significant progress, made during the 1990s, was an agreement on the demarcation of the Tonkin Gulf with Vietnam, a demarcation that, significantly, corresponded almost entirely with China's nine-dashed line.

But what that decade also brought about was greater Chinese leverage. On the one hand, it became increasingly clear that ASEAN was divided. In 1997, for instance, Vietnam could not obtain support for denouncing Chinese exploration activities on its continental shelf. Claimed the Malaysian Defense Minister Syed Hamid Albar: "We in Southeast Asia generally feel that China has so far been a sober and responsible regional player. Its advocacy of joint exploration of South China Sea resources with other regional states and its recent indication of readiness to abide by the international law in resolving the Spratly's issue have made us feel that it wants to coexist in peace with its neighbours." The ASEAN countries also remained divided over the necessity of a Code of Conduct for the South China Sea. China was against such a code and argued that it was better to have bilateral codes with the different claimants. The Philippines and Vietnam continued to lobby for a regional code, but they did not receive the support of Malaysia and disagreed among themselves about whether the code should be limited to the Spratly Islands, which were claimed by four ASEAN members, and the Paracel or Xisha Islands, which were claimed only by Vietnam. On the other hand, China had become much more present in the area. By the late 1990s, it had by far the largest fishing fleet and its emerging oil industries had started to gain important knowhow in offshore drilling. China also readied for a major push in its naval capabilities. During most of the 1990s, the South Fleet was limited to a frail backbone of 14 Jianghu frigates and eight Luda destroyers. But the order for Russian destroyers and submarines, as well as the commissioning of a new type of frigate and destroyer, the Jiangwei II and the Luhai, in 1999 spearheaded the fast naval modernization of the following decades.

The Cross-Straits Relations

Further north, Taiwan emerged on the horizon as the biggest obstacle. It is true that 1989 was the year that Taiwanese officials stopped referring to Chinese politicians as "communist bandits." That was not only symbolically important. It also reflected Taipei's growing confidence, confidence that in turn permitted a more relaxed attitude towards the mainland. The Tiananmen crisis did cause some protest, but even the largest manifestation, a spiritual shield for the Chinese students before the presidential palace, did not mobilize more than 10,000 people. For the rest, Taiwan remained remarkably prudent. Since the travel ban was lifted in 1987, over 900,000 Taiwanese had travelled to the mainland. This encouraged companies to explore investment projects, but also made Taiwanese citizens more appreciative of the increasing freedoms that they had come to enjoy since the lifting of Taiwan's martial law in 1987. In 1989, a poll showed that only 52 percent of the Taiwanese considered their national identity to be Chinese. Exactly because Taiwan grew more confident about its own transition, it became more relaxed towards China.[20] "The more you see on the mainland, the more you treasure what you have in Taiwan," said the Deputy Secretary General of the Kuomintang. Taiwan confirmed its intention to participate in the Asian Games and also considered allowing officials to participate in exchanges with the mainland. As another gesture of confidence, Taiwan's defense budget was trimmed significantly in 1990. Ten days after the Tiananmen crisis, President Lee Teng Hui proposed four principles to deal with the mainland, their main message being that any negotiations about a future settlement should be agreed on an equal footing.[21] Taipei also stopped its self-defeating habit of abruptly ending all relations with countries that shifted diplomatic recognition to Beijing and opted for an "elastic policy" instead. During most of the 1990s, Beijing scarcely moved away from its firm and often even nervous posturing. Ahead of the presidential elections of 1990, it warned of repercussions if the Democratic Progressive Party were to win. It turned down offers to establish official contacts, asking direct trade to be established first and fiercely resisting Taiwan's application for membership of the GATT. Taiwan continued to make new concessions. In 1992, for instance, it allowed banks to work directly with their Chinese counterparts to facilitate trade.

Only in January 1995 did Beijing come up with a more pragmatic vision for managing cross-straits relations. In his eight proposals for reunification, Jiang Zemin asserted that political differences should not affect or interfere with the economic cooperation.[22] These proposals were lost somewhat in the Taiwanese legislative elections of that year and the presidential elections of 1996. In 1995 and 1996, China held missile tests and amphibious exercises in response to Lee Teng Hui's visit to the United States. Talks restarted soon afterwards. In 1996, shipping standards were established to facilitate trade. In 1997, the ban on direct trade was eased. In April 1997, direct shipping between Fuzhou and Xiamen on the mainland and

Kaohsiung in Taiwan was started. In March 1998, a regular container shipping route was inaugurated across the Straits. Relations would remain calm until another stormy election campaign in 2000.

Korea and Japan

An important breakthrough was made with South Korea. In the late 1990s, Seoul overcame its initial reluctance, mostly because of economic interests. Its large companies feared missing business opportunities if ties were not officially restored. An important signal, South Korean firms offered millions in sponsorship in the run-up to the Asian Games in China. In June 1989, Seoul approved a first Chinese company to invest directly in the country – to produce televisions. Beijing reciprocated by allowing Korean Airlines to fly to Beijing for the 11th Asian Games. In October 1989, the two sides agreed to exchange trade offices. Initially, China refused to allow the office to be located in its capital until the establishment of full political relations, but it gave in. In 1992, diplomatic relations were finally established, but for the remainder of the decade ties would be rocked by the nuclear nationalism of Pyongyang, which reached its temporary peak with the long-range missile launch in 1998. Negotiations would swing back and forth until 2003, when North Korea withdrew from the Non-Proliferation Treaty. Throughout this process, Seoul repeatedly vented its displeasure at China's reluctance to exert pressure on the regime of Kim Yong-Il.

North Korea also became a bone of contention between Beijing and Tokyo, but there were other, more important resentments. In the first three years after the Tiananmen crisis, relations developed steadily. Japan's exports to China had leapt from US$8 billion in 1989 to US$16 billion in 1992, making China the second largest export market after the United States. 1992 was also the year that Jiang Zemin visited Japan and Emperor Akihito paid an official six-day visit to China, the first time a Japanese Emperor had visited China in the thousand years of history of the two nations. "It was a tense journey," a Japanese diplomat recollected, "The emperor had to walk a tightrope between the desire of China to obtain an apology for the past and the Japanese public opinion that did not tolerate humiliation."[23] From a Chinese viewpoint, the gains were significant: domestic prestige, recognition of China's growing power, and confirmation that China had important friends at a time when its reputation was questioned in other parts of the world.

But even if that visit was supposed to turn a page in the history of the two countries, Beijing's red lines did not change at all. The first such red line remained China's objection to Japan's sovereignty over the Senkaku or Diaoyu Islands. That was made plain with the passing of the Law of the Territorial Sea, which claimed the islands to be part of China, even if Jiang Zemin reassured Japan of the commitment to shelve the issue. In 1993, two survey ships were dispatched to the exclusive economic zone around the islands; 15 survey ships went in 1994.[24] In 1995, Japanese fighters made a first scramble against Chinese jets. In 1996, Beijing responded bitterly to a law that asserted Japan's exclusive economic zone around the islands. From then onwards, tensions over the area continued to increase. A second red line was drawn against Japan's militarization and that line was increasingly flouted. Japan did not only participate in the Gulf War, polls also showed a majority of citizens willing to scrap the pacifist article nine from the constitution. In the 1990s, Japan carried out an impressive overhaul of its armed forces. Between 1990 and 2002 it commissioned no less than 15 destroyers, 5 corvettes, 3 large landing ships, and 5 attack submarines – with 6 more to follow. It started building 94 modern variants of the F-16, and purchased 4 long-range warning and control aircraft, and 178 Seahawk helicopters for hunting submarines. With its military modernization, Japan was also crossing a third red line: it allowed the

United States to expand its military presence on its territory. That presence was affirmed in a Mutual Security Treaty, signed by President Bill Clinton in 1996. On top of that, Japan signed an agreement with the United States to conduct joint technology research on theater missile defense. If the military balance was shifting in the East China Sea, it was shifting to China's detriment. This all led to deep frustration, indicated most visibly by Jiang Zemin's eagerness to raise the issue of Japan's aggressive past at every possible gathering. More importantly, it added to China's determination to balance Japan – both economically and militarily. The consequences, however, would only become visible after the turn of the century.

The Crumbling Empire

Then there was Russia. When the Chinese leaders received Mikhail Gorbachev in the Great Hall of the People, he had to come in through the back door because protesters in Tiananmen Square had blocked the front door. The meeting was historic. Even if Beijing was up in arms, Deng Xiaoping must have felt that the tables were turning. A month before Gorbachev left, the Soviets were confronted with their own protests, in Tbilisi. Dramatic rates of inflation plagued most of Eastern Europe. As they conferred and gave toasts, trainloads of tanks rattled over the border of Mongolia, back to their Siberian bases. Missiles were being withdrawn from the border. China had a dying rival empire almost on its knees. The new Chinese leadership only needed to get the most out of its demise. By January 1990, Moscow had pulled all its Mig-23 fighter planes back from Vietnam. Moscow accepted the first important Chinese mining projects on its soil and border talks were restarted. In comparison to China's maritime territorial disputes and the boundary conflict with India, the demarcation of the border with Russia was fairly straightforward. There was an agreement from 1896 that served as a reference point and most of the border consisted of natural barriers like rivers and watersheds. Until 1989 China had requested settlement of all issues at once, but dropped this demand for a section-by-section approach. In the first agreement, of 1991, Russia yielded 700 islands and 1,500 hectares of land to China.[25] It also gave China the right to use the border rivers for shipping.[26] In a second agreement, in 1994, a short disputed section between Mongolia and Kazakhstan was settled. That left three islands – the Bolshoi Ussuriysk or Heixiazi, the Tarabarov or Yinlong, and the Abagaitu Shoal – for which a consensus would only be reached in 2004.

If the Tiananmen protests were still a humbling experience for China, Russia learned to be humble in the decade that followed. Already in 1992 President Boris Yeltsin had had to cut short a visit to Beijing because of new political problems at home.[27] Also that year, China's gross domestic product and industrial output surpassed those of Russia. The crumbling empire proved a useful partner for China to advance its broader strategic interests, like the creation of a multipolar order and the constraining of the remaining superpower. If Beijing at first supported Western action against Iraq's invasion of Kuwait, Beijing and Moscow soon started to criticize the United States for trying to control the Middle East and other forms of American interference – in the Balkans, in Eastern Europe, and in Eastern Asia.[28] The two also supported each other in resisting Western liberal values and highlighting the importance of sovereignty in regard to attempts at secession, whether those came from fighters in Chechnya, protesters in Xinjiang, or politicians in Taiwan. The joint statement of 1997 contained all of China's sticking points: "A growing number of countries are beginning to recognize the need for mutual respect, equality and mutual advantage," it stated. "Every country has the right independently to choose its path of development in the light of its own specific conditions and without interference from other states."[29] At least as important was the fact that a weak

Russia became more helpful in strengthening China's power. As was the case with Japan, high-level visits contributed to Beijing's prestige, but Russia also became China's most important supplier of military hardware, technology, and raw materials. That was also the main challenge. Russia was anxious to work with China, but, as one Chinese official confided, "much of that cooperation was a fig leaf for Russia's own decline and we could not yet afford to allow it to fall off."[30]

One way in which China confronted Russia with its weakness was by filling up the void left in Mongolia and Central Asia after the implosion of the Soviet Union. As Moscow had to cut its aid to Mongolia, Ulaanbaatar reached out to new friends – the United States, Japan, and China. China first of all wanted to make sure that Mongolia remained neutral and to mitigate the fears in Ulaanbaatar about a possible recolonization of the country. In 1994 it achieved this in an agreement stating that: "Neither Party will allow a third country to use its territory which may adversely affect the state sovereignty and security of the other Party."[31] From then onwards, China's influence grew rapidly. If in 1994 China took only 16 percent of Mongolia's exports, this increased to 54 percent in 2003. China also became a major investor in the mining sector and broke Russia's monopoly as a supplier of refined petroleum products.[32]

In Central Asia, Russia's influence was dwindling as well, but mostly to the benefit of the West, Iran, and Turkey.[33] Western multinationals secured the largest part of the oil contracts and also took a growing part of the region's exports. By 2003, for instance, the share of China and Russia in the total exports of Kazakhstan, Kyrgyzstan, Tajikistan, Uzbekistan, and Turkmenistan was not more than 12 and 16 percent, respectively. Most of the countries, especially Kazakhstan, were keen on business, but had doubts about China's long-term intentions and criticized the treatment of ethnic minorities in the Autonomous Region of Xinjiang. Kazakhstan led an offensive to tie

China to its policy of military restraint, asking for a formal statement to provide security guarantees in 1995. That year also, it lodged formal protests, together with Kyrgyzstan and Uzbekistan, against China's nuclear tests in Lop Nor. It worked in lockstep with Russia, Kyrgyzstan and Tajikistan to get China to sign the 1996 agreement on military confidence building in the border area. The same year, the Chinese planning commission proposed a Pan-Asian energy bridge, connecting Central Asia with the Pacific. Chinese firms made concrete proposals, but the Kazakh government showed itself heedful of overdependence.[34] But, after a slow decade, China had laid the foundations of a much bigger footprint. The Central Asian countries guaranteed China that they would combat Islamic terrorism and constrain secessionists from Xinjiang. With the establishment of the Shanghai Cooperation Organisation (SCO), the successor of the Shanghai Five, China had created an acceptable forum to convey proposals to the region – and to give added weight to its decisions without causing too much distrust.

Strategic Opportunity

Just before his retirement as president, at the 16th Party Congress in 2002, Jiang Zemin argued that China had entered a period of strategic opportunity, during which relative international stability, peace, and economic growth gave China the chance to build a well-off society.[35] "It facilitates companies' access to more capital, especially direct investment from multinationals, which will enable them to speed up their economic development and restructuring," Jiang clarified. "It encourages them to acquire and exploit new markets and develop foreign trade and economic cooperation with other countries by giving full play to their advantages. Furthermore, it enables them to acquire advanced technologies and management expertise more quickly so that they will be able to make better use of their advantages as late starters and attain technological progress by leaps and bounds."[36]

Under Jiang, China's diplomacy spared no effort to seize that period of opportunity. Tangibly even, one could witness the transformation. The foreign service became larger, younger, and brighter. It learned to talk the talk and walk the walk. Chinese embassies in all Asian countries continued to expand, and so did the centers of diplomacy in Beijing. Many of the sturdy headquarters along the Chang'an Avenue, the main road that passes by the Forbidden City, including those of the International Department of the Communist Party and the Ministry of Commerce, were built during that period. The Ministry of Foreign Affairs opened its new building at Chaoyangmen Outer Street in 1996 and would soon be surrounded by the posh office buildings of oil companies, banks, and trading companies. Most Asian countries enlarged, or at least embellished, their embassies in the Sanlitun area, the small ones, like Laos and Cambodia, even supported by the Chinese government.

The neighborhood policy broadened and became much more proactive. China took one initiative after the other, especially in regard to commerce and low politics. It did so in both bilateral and multilateral settings. No doubt that window of opportunity was the result of China's changing environment. If China succeeded in attracting the attention of the growing number of Japanese, Taiwanese, and Western companies that searched for cheap labor in the 1980s, it managed to consolidate its position as a manufacturing hub throughout the 1990s. The accession to the World Trade Organization certainly helped with that. By the turn of the century, it had overwhelmed its two main peer competitors, India and Southeast Asia. Japan and South Korea were starting to feel the heat in low-end industries. At the strategic level, the Soviet Union disappeared as a challenger, India relatively weakened, and ASEAN as a block was not to be feared. The world tended towards multipolarity, but one factor stood in the way:

America's military predominance and its blatant unilateralism. In Asia this remained particularly worrisome in tandem with a re-militarizing Japan and loomed over China's geopolitical weak spot – its coast. But, again, the regional order had started to change. The balance of power was in motion. This was no reason for euphoria, no reason for complacency, and certainly no reason for diplomatic adventurism or escalating territorial disputes, but it gave China more confidence to follow the course of reform, gradual opening up, and strategic self-restraint. It was revisionism at its best: quiet and effective.

− 5 −

Peaceful Development

Nine years after the Tiananmen crisis, Jiang Zemin stood in the Great Hall of the People, next to the infamous square, before dozens of journalists, and with President Bill Clinton at his side. No back doors this time. Beaming with confidence, smiling and joking, the President sparred with his American counterpart on issues that ranged from economic reforms to human rights. Jiang's self-assured attitude came as no surprise. His guests could witness how thousands of construction workers were transforming the skyline of Beijing into a pincushion of apartment blocks. In Shanghai, skyscrapers had replaced the mosquito-infested marshes of Pudong. Between 1989 and the turn of the century, the Chinese economy grew on average by 10 percent per year. With that performance it dwarfed its neighbors. China's share in Asia's total economic output increased from 6 percent in 1989 to 19 percent in 2002, its share in the region's industrial production from 8 to 28 percent, its share in Asia's exports from 6 to 19 percent, and its part in the inflows of foreign direct investments from 16 to 55 percent. Japan remained stuck in stagnation, India got nowhere with its ambitions for industrialization, and the benefits of Southeast Asia's growth were largely wiped out by inflation.[1] Much of China's backyard was plagued by social unrest and secessionist movements. "Besides a glide in the growth of exports, investment and consumption remained strong," the *People's Daily* bragged. "The expansion of domestic demand had not only cleared the outstanding accounts in domestic infrastructure construction, improved people's living standards, supported the sustained, rapid development of the Chinese economy, but also has provided the Chinese economy with more room for maneuver in the turbulent world economy."[2]

And still, China's quest for power and prosperity was far from over. In a 2002 survey, only 50 percent of the Chinese appeared to be satisfied with the economic situation. The Ministry of Public Security reported that there were as many as 40,000 mass incidents in 2000, up from 8,700 in 1993. In 2001, a research group working for the Party's Central Committee warned that China's ramshackle economic development could "bring growing dangers and pressures" and that "the number of group incidents may jump, severely harming social stability and even disturbing the smooth implementation of reform and opening up."[3] The expansion of foreign companies also led to nervousness. In 2002, 25 percent of China's industrial output and 45 percent of its exports were generated by foreign firms. Opinion leaders and decision makers started to warn against becoming too dependent on globalization. "Globalization is a double edged sword which can help break through the brambles and thorns, but may also harm the servant," Peking University's Wang Yizhou posited. "In this context a new security concept should be established that pays equal attention to economic, social and political aspects."[4] Zhang Boli, a Deputy Director of the Department of Economics of the Central Committee, put it as follows: "Globalization is still a reflection of the old unfair and irrational international order and has further aggravated the polarization between rich and poor."[5]

The security environment became more complicated too. India and Japan both justified leaps in their defense budgets by referring to the China threat.[6] Japanese newspapers announced plans to build a 40,000-ton carrier by 2015 and to purchase over two hundred F-15 fighter jets. But the largest challenge still came from the United States. The 2001 *Quadrennial Defense Review* shifted the attention from the Atlantic to the Pacific. The 2002 *National Security Strategy* claimed that China was following an outdated path by pursuing advanced military capabilities that threatened its neighbors.[7] Especially since the Taiwan Missile Crisis of 1996, Washington had been building up its military presence in the region. Since the 1990s, 10 modernized Los Angeles-class submarines have been assigned to the Seventh Fleet, together with 18 modern Arleigh Burke-class destroyers. The US also showed its resolve by continuing to send planes and vessels into China's exclusive economic zone. After the commissioning of a new generation of towed array sensor ships, it started new efforts to map the seafloor around China. Military exchanges were set up with Central Asia and Mongolia. With Centrazbat 97, the North Atlantic Treaty Organization (NATO) pushed its presence right up to China's western doorstep. And that presence further increased after the 9/11 terrorist attacks. "An overview of the current global reality reveals that the Cold War mentality still lingers on and hegemonism and power politics manifest themselves from time to time," Jiang Zemin complained. "The tendency towards closer military alliance is on the rise. New forms of gunboat policy are rampant. Regional conflicts have cropped up one after another."[8] The mood further deteriorated as a consequence of the release of a report of the House of Representatives, the Cox Report, that accused China of stealing military technology, and the collision between a Chinese fighter jet and an American EP-3 patrol plane in 2001.

Five days after Hu Jintao took over the reins, on March 19, 2003, this perception was rudely confirmed by Washington's decision to invade Iraq. The United States brushed aside the request of Beijing, Moscow, and Paris to try harder to find a diplomatic solution. Meanwhile, Defense Minister Donald Rumsfeld was trumpeting regime change in North Korea. The same Rumsfeld had earlier declared, together with a group of other neoconservatives, that America needed to increase its military pressure on China, "providing the spur to the process of democratization in China."[9] But 2003 was also another year that showed China's confidence. It became the world's largest exporter of manufactured goods and was selected to host the 2010 World Expo in Shanghai. China opened the Three Gorges Dam, resumed works on the Shanghai World Financial Center, broke ground for the world's largest shipyard, started building the world's longest bridge, took the world's longest oil pipeline into operation, and, not least, launched its first manned space mission. America's unilateralism and the consequent frustration among other countries also formed a new opportunity for China to highlight its peaceful intentions. "The only choice for China under the current international situation is to rise peacefully," Zheng Bijian stated in 2003 at the Boao Forum, China's beachside equivalent of the World Economic Forum. That year's session of the Forum was almost designed for Asian leaders to reject the China threat and subscribe to the doctrine of peaceful rise.

The next year on Jade Belt Beach, President Hu Jintao explained his policy priorities for Asia. The baseline remained that China's development contributed to peace. Hu reiterated that China would treat all countries as equals and try to settle disputes through dialogue. He also promised more political exchanges, the deepening of economic linkages through trade, investment, free trade arrangements, the strengthening of regional economic institutions and macro-economic coordination, broader people-to-people exchanges, and more frequent military-to-military cooperation. The fresh political hosts of the 2004 Boao Forum could back those assertions up with several recent important achievements. In 2003, China had signed the Treaty of Amity and Cooperation and a free trade agreement with ASEAN. With India it had signed a Declaration on Principles for Relations and Comprehensive Cooperation. Beijing trod carefully after Japan's Prime Minister Junichiro Koizumi visited the Yasukuni Shrine in the spring of 2003. Harsh statements of the Ministry of Foreign Affairs notwithstanding, Premier Wen Jiabao shook hands with Koizumi on the sidelines of the ASEAN summit and advanced a series of priorities for cooperation. Most significantly, however, China had hosted the first six-party talks, touting its "creatively designed hexagonal negotiation table around which all delegates participated as equals" and its "comfortable couches in four corners" for informal gatherings.[10]

The Fourth Generation would be remembered even more than the Third Generation for the maturing of China's Asia policy, the rapid deepening of economic relations, the proliferation of bilateral and multilateral dialogues, and the desire to turn non-traditional security threats, like piracy and terrorism, into an opportunity for confidence building and cooperation. As China developed its narrative of peaceful development, a growing number of China watchers identified this as a confirmation of a more profound transformation of China's foreign policy, its strategic calculations, and even its identity. Posited the American professor-diplomat Susan Shirk: "What distinguishes the Chinese approach is its willingness to accommodate the interests of its neighbors in order to build trust and increase Chinese influence."[11] But, again, that willingness to accommodate was limited, as we can witness from three important issues in Sino–Asian relations: territorial disputes, Taiwan, and trade.

Southeast Asia and the South China Sea

Southeast Asia remained the cornerstone of China's neighborhood policy. At the time of China's leadership change, the region was still struggling with the fallout of the financial crisis and plagued by growing violence in Indonesia, the Philippines, Thailand, and Myanmar. In all these matters, ASEAN remained an ineffective and marginal player. The association also failed to make progress in establishing a free trade area. An important deadline for a consensus on non-tariff barriers in 2005 was missed and it did not succeed in removing tariff barriers by the agreed deadline of 2010. Instead, member states preferred bilateral trade agreements with large economies outside the region. A report by an Eminent Persons Group that argued for stronger institutions and more stringent rules to guide integration fell largely on deaf ears. "The regional project often got more support from China than from our own governments," it read.[12] Nevertheless, ASEAN remained important for China. ASEAN multilateralism provided a useful cover for the pursuit of bilateral negotiations with its smaller members. In fact, China faced an almost ideal situation. ASEAN was too weak to form a counterweight against China, but it was still visible enough to give the impression that it was in charge. "Two things are important to keep our neighbors at ease: one is the military predominance of the United States, the other is the prospect of regional cooperation," a researcher at the China Academy of Social Sciences explained. "We are more confident about the second."[13]

The South China Sea continued to catch a lot of attention in the Sino–ASEAN exchanges and in those relations intransigence remained Beijing's trademark. In May 2009, 60 years after Premier Zhou Enlai put forward the map with the nine-dashed line, the Chinese government submitted to the United Nations a new map of the South China Sea – with almost exactly the same nine-dashed line. "China has indisputable sovereignty over the islands in the South China Sea and the adjacent waters," it explicated to the Secretary General, "and enjoys sovereign rights and jurisdiction over the relevant waters as well as the seabed and subsoil thereof."[14] Moreover, countries like Malaysia, Vietnam, the Philippines, and Brunei, conveyed to the

United Nations that they would only claim the territorial sea 12 miles around the islands in the South China Sea and not the exclusive economic zone of 200 miles. China made no such concession and interventions in the area seemed to demonstrate that it was going for the full exclusive economic zone.[15] The same attitude prevailed in regard to the possibility of involving countries from outside the region and international organizations. China continued to resist such possibilities.

But if the core of China's agenda remained static, three important changes became apparent. A first change was the new upsurge in dialogues; dialogues, however, that did not make the slightest difference in settling the dispute. The Declaration on the Conduct of Parties in the South China Sea was signed in November 2002 and gave way to a series of senior official meetings, called SOMs by insiders, whose main achievement was to establish yet another series of meetings, the so-called joint working groups. Later on, China proposed to establish yet another platform: the Eminent Persons and Expert Working Group. The Declaration itself was deliberately kept vague by China. And even the most specific article, article 5, which called for self-restraint and refraining from the action of inhabiting the presently uninhabited islands, was interpreted loosely. Between "inhabiting" and doing nothing there remained, after all, a whole range of options: erecting markers, extending landing strips, building bird-watching towers, and much more.[16] The same was true of article 6: "Pending a comprehensive and durable settlement of the disputes, the parties concerned may explore or undertake cooperative activities." That did not, of course, exclude unilateral activities, and that leads us to a second change: China gathered more capabilities to increase its presence within the legal imbroglio. With the commissioning of new destroyers, frigates, submarines, and missile boats the navy could show its flag more convincingly, with the major exercise of 2010 clearly being a turning point. The coastguard and other constabulary agencies expanded, together with China's fleet of modern fishing boats and surveying vessels. The commissioning of deep-water drilling rig CNOOC 981 confirmed China's energy ambitions in the South China Sea. "Large-scale deep-water rigs are our mobile national territory and a strategic weapon," Chairman Wang Yilin reportedly said.

On the other hand, and this was the third change, internal divisions became more damaging to the credibility of ASEAN. China had not forgotten the disagreements in the negotiations ahead of the Declaration and also in the years afterwards, and those quarrels persisted. This was not least because territorial tensions intensified among the ASEAN members themselves. At the ASEAN Regional Forum in July 2010, Cambodia, Laos, Myanmar, and Thailand did not back other countries in criticizing China. That year, the Cambodian President Hun Sen rebuked attempts by Vietnam and the Philippines to use ASEAN to corner China. "The issue should not be internationalized or multilateralized," he stressed. Discord reached its climax in 2012.[17] In April of that year, two Chinese surveillance ships prevented Filipino authorities from arresting Chinese fishermen for collecting illegal species near to the Scarborough Shoal. Even if that caused an outcry, China held on. It deployed a frigate and sent 30 fishing boats to demonstrate its determination. Meanwhile, Cambodia resisted attempts by Manila to mention the incident in a communiqué of the ASEAN foreign affairs ministers, which caused their summit to break down. Explained the Cambodian Foreign Minister Hor Namhong: "I have told my colleagues that the meeting of the ASEAN foreign ministers is not a court, a place to give a verdict about the dispute." Indonesia and Malaysia initially stood by Hanoi and Manila, but that support was short-lived. In an interview, the Malaysian Defense Minister said that he was not worried about China's intentions. "Just because you have enemies, doesn't mean your enemies are my enemies." China did not really gain from all this, but it did prevent diplomatic resistance to its growing presence.

Japan and India

Relations with Japan did not fare any better. The two countries entered a tense period of adjustment, with Japan also having to come to grips with the shifting balance of power. In 2004, China's official defense budget surpassed that of Japan. In 2012, China surpassed Japan as the second largest economy. That coincided with the start of a rapid modernization of its military presence in the East China Sea. Between 2003 and 2012, the East Sea Fleet commissioned four potent Russian destroyers, six new frigates of the Jiankai family, four Russian Kilo-class submarines, and three Song-class submarines. Trade relations further expanded, investment flows surged, and the number of bilateral dialogues increased, but no progress was made on the most divisive issue – history. As Premier Koizumi persisted in visiting the Yasukuni Shrine, China persisted in responding bitterly. Tensions flared up when a new Japanese history book was published that did not go far enough in admitting Japan's imperialistic atrocities. It was in such disputes that China's growing clout became manifest. Threats of boycotts and deliberate customs delays made Japanese companies nervous. Beijing did not, therefore, become more sensitive or less tolerant. Its responses remained very predictable, but it had more weight to throw around.

That also applied to the territorial dispute. As in the previous few decades, Beijing rejected Japan's ownership of the Senkaku or Diaoyu Islands and the median line as the proposed dividing line between the exclusive economic zones in the East China Sea. But now it had two important instruments to show its resolve: its large oil companies and its navy. Those oil companies, CNOOC and Sinopec, eyed a large stretch of the floor of the East China Sea. In a part of this area, where the Senkaku or Diaoyu Islands are also located, the Chinese and Japanese exclusive economic zones overlap. China did not start any drilling here, but it did so just outside Japan's median line. One of the gas fields, Pinghu, is still 35 kilometers away. Production at the Pinghu field began in April 1999 with gas piped to Shanghai and Ningbo through a pipeline that Japan even helped to finance. But there are seven other fields, much closer to Japan's claimed exclusive economic zone: Chunxiao, Tianwaitian, Duanqiao, Baoyunting, Canxue, Longjing, and Wuyunting. In 2003, China started drilling in Chunxiao, which is only 4 kilometers from Japan's claimed exclusive economic zone. Trade Minister Shoichi Nakagawa made the problem clear to a Chinese delegation by dropping two straws in a glass of orange juice, stating that China was sucking out all the gas from a field that stretched into Japan's exclusive economic zone. "The platforms are in China, but the gas is in Japan." China consequently proposed joint development, but only on the Japanese side of the median line. In 2008, after 12 rounds of negotiations, Tokyo and Beijing signed a memorandum on joint development in the East China Sea. Japanese officials initially hailed it as a victory, but the area identified for cooperation was small. Besides Longjing, it excluded the contentious gas fields. China allowed Japanese companies to participate in its other fields, but only if they recognized its sovereignty. In 2009, China began to develop the Tianwaitian gas field unilaterally. Tokyo threatened to file a complaint to the International Tribunal for the Law of the Sea, but Beijing did not budge. Drilling in Chunxiao and Tianwaitian went on and the joint development block was left untouched.

At the same time, the Chinese navy became more eager to show the flag and more capable of doing so. Until then, it did not have many options to match the Japanese patrols along the median line, the frequent passages of American warships, and the exercises that both countries held in the East China Sea. In 2004, Tokyo also announced that the Japanese coastguard would administer the Senkaku Islands. The Joint Agreement with the United States of 2005 flagged the status of Taiwan as a matter of mutual concern and only added to China's perception of being pressured by the Japanese–American naval axis. That changed. In 2003 and 2004, Chinese submarines for the first time ventured near to Japanese territorial waters. In 2003, China deployed five navy ships east of the median line. In 2005, a Chinese navy destroyer aimed its guns at a Japanese maritime self-defense force surveillance plane. The Chinese navy also started long-range patrols through important Japanese maritime corridors. These corridors are international waters, but China refuses to accept Japan's request to be informed in advance whenever military ships use them. In 2008, four Chinese naval vessels passed through the Tsugaru Strait. In 2010, two submarines and eight destroyers sailed through the Miyako Strait. In 2012, three navy ships passed through the Osumi Strait. An important signal, some of these voyages to the Western Pacific ended in exercises near Okinotorishima. Even though China has no claim on that tiny islet itself, it refuses to recognize it as an island around which Japan can claim an exclusive economic zone.[18] Okinotorishima is a strategically vital island. Japan claims several other islands in its vicinity, but if Okinotorishima were added, Tokyo thinks it can claim an exclusive economic zone that stretches from Hokkaido all the way to the American island Guam. Okinotorishima is thus really the keystone in what could be a formidable legal barrier to China entering the Pacific Ocean, at least if one accepts the Japanese claim and follows China's traditional argument that an exclusive economic zone requires passing navies to ask for permission of the country that owns it.

Given the unlikely presence of warships in the high ranges of the Himalayas, the signaling of China's claims along the border with India was less dramatic. It was mostly limited to leaving empty packs of cigarettes and painted signs in disputed areas. China and India took several new initiatives to avoid escalation. In 2002, maps of a part of the border were exchanged. In 2003, a landmark agreement was signed that set out the goals and guiding principles of the relationship between the two countries. The Natu La Pass, a corridor at 4,000 meters, was reopened. Premier Wen Jiabao spoke of "mountains of peace." But it could not be. In the following years, news media on both sides reported one incident after another: transgressions of patrols, boats on disputed mountain lakes and helicopter incursions. At the same time, both sides spared no efforts to expand their presence in the barren area. While new Chinese facilities received most of the attention, India was at least as fast in unfolding a flimsy maze of dusty border patrol roads, punctuated with shelters and observation posts. By 2012, India had many more military hubs along the western part of the line of actual control – mostly in Shyok Valley, around the Pangon Tso Lake, and further south – than China. The same was true in the eastern sector. China apparently opted for a different approach. The number of border patrols might have been stepped up, but more important was that it modernized major facilities a few hundred miles away from the frontier – air force bases, tactical missile facilities, and railway stations that served as platforms for the vast contingents of armed forces deeper in its hinterland. China also promoted economic development along important border rivers like the Sengge, the Yarlung Tsangpo, and the Xibaxa Qu. At the same time, neither side made significant concessions. In 2005, China formally recognized Sikkim as a part of India, but that was hardly a concession. Moreover, Beijing first managed to get India to recognize Tibet as a part of China. China still refused to relinquish small pockets of territory like Tawang, Demchock, Kaurik, and Skipki La. In 2011 and 2012, new measures were put in place to avoid incidents, but these were to no avail. New incursions sent public emotions to a new high. That also explains why the most plausible deal, of swapping the 90,000 square kilometers of Arunachal Pradesh, controlled by India, for the 38,000 square kilometers of Aksai China, could not materialize. "Any such swap," a Chinese diplomat avowed, "would be political suicide on the Indian side and very badly received on the Chinese side."[19]

Relations with Taiwan

In Taiwan, China was confronted with a defiant president who tried to survive in a context of economic uncertainty. Partially as a consequence of the bursting of the dotcom bubble in the United States, Taiwan had slid into a recession and unemployment soared.[20] The worse the economy got, the more fiercely President Chen Sui-Bian accused the mainland of using its short-range missiles – "state-sponsored terrorism" he called it – to coerce Taiwan into unification. In 2003, he promised a referendum on cross-straits relations. Even though Chen got re-elected in 2004, his referendum got nowhere and his opponents in the Kuomintang gained significantly in the parliament. Equally important, Washington refused to sign off on an important delivery of destroyers with missile defense capacity. During the previous years, it had also become clear that the Taiwanese business community was so heavily invested in the mainland that it emerged as a tireless lobby for restraint. To stabilize cross-straits relations, President Hu Jintao proposed a "two-handed strategy" that combined a firm component – including a political curfew around President Chen, diplomatic isolation, and military power – with a soft component that left the door open for negotiations with the Kuomintang Party and more economic exchanges. This was reaffirmed in the Anti-Secession Law of 2005. The law asserted the one-China principle, proposed more exchanges, but also reserved the use of force should Taiwan claim independence. Especially the last clause ruffled feathers in Taipei, but the one-China principle also deliberately left the options open about Taiwan's final status in a reunified China.[21] Moreover, the emphasis shifted from promoting reunification to opposing unilateral independence and – temporarily – maintaining the status quo. Barely a month after the ratification, China invited Lien Chan, the chairman of the Kuomintang, for a meeting with the top leadership in the Great Hall of the

People in Beijing. The joint communiqué that followed the visit called for all-round cross-strait economic cooperation and even a common market. Both sides vowed to open up direct sea and air links, strengthen investment and trade, and boost agricultural cooperation. As early as July, Beijing announced that it would scrap import tariffs on 15 types of Taiwanese fruit. A few months later, it offered a US$30 billion loan to Taiwanese investors in China and approved over-flight rights for Taiwanese air carriers.

In the following years, China consistently followed a double-track strategy, while the balance of power gradually altered to its benefit. Hundreds of short-range missiles were now deployed as a powerful deterrent, and while Taiwan's navy became outdated, China ramped up its capacity to close down the Taiwan Strait, thanks to its maturing navy and a rapidly growing core of modern fighter jets in its air force. It also weathered the impact of the global financial crisis well, whereas the Taiwanese economy nosedived into another recession in 2008. That gave China much more confidence to support the Kuomintang during the presidential elections of 2008. Ma Ying-jeou, who won the ballot, made economic development and commercial cooperation with the mainland the linchpin of his campaign and Beijing indirectly tried to throw as much weight onto the electoral scales as possible. After the financial crisis erupted in 2008, it immediately pledged US$19 billion of loans to Taiwanese companies. By late 2008, the "three links" were largely established with the signing of four agreements on air transport, direct sea transport, postal cooperation, and food safety.[22] As a result, the number of mainlanders that visited Taiwan, mostly tourists, almost quadrupled to one million in 2009. In January 2009, both sides were informally testing the waters for a Comprehensive Economic Partnership Agreement.[23] "We will try our best in everything that will benefit the Taiwan compatriots, and we will honor our words," President Hu Jintao stated in a meeting with Taiwanese business leaders on the potential economic agreement. "During the negotiation process, we will put into full consideration the interests of Taiwan compatriots, especially those of farmers."[24]

The emphasis on farmers had much political significance, as most of the Taiwanese agriculture is located in the south, a stronghold of the China-skeptical Democratic Progressive Party. Wang Yi in his turn announced that China was willing to make five concessions: to ask for fewer "early harvest" items than Taiwan, to consider the interests of smaller Taiwanese companies, not to exhaust weak Taiwanese industries, to make a gesture toward Taiwanese farmers, and not to push for labor exports to Taiwan. The Economic Cooperation Framework Agreement (ECFA), signed in June 2010, rolled out an action plan for the development of a free trade area.[25] It provided for an important early harvest scheme that lowered trade barriers for a large number of goods and services. With ECFA Beijing demonstrated its willingness to make compromises. Whereas Taiwan vowed to lower tariffs on 267 items, China included 539 items in its early harvest offer, including agricultural products, petrochemicals, machinery, transport equipment, and textiles. Taiwan did not include farming products in its list and also offered a much smaller package of tariff reductions for manufactured goods. China unilaterally opened important services markets like insurance, medical services, IT, accounting, and securities trading. In 2010, Chinese procurement missions – mostly composed of a provincial government with a delegation of local companies – placed orders worth US$15 billion, good for US$652 in potential revenues per capita.[26] China's main gain was stability. It is clear that Beijing, in spite of its military clout in the Taiwan Strait, was not yet ready for a confrontation at the risk of defeat and at the expense of its economic growth. For the rest, the achievements of the trade with Taiwan were not so obvious. It did attract more Taiwanese investment, US$75 billion by 2009, and elicited a greater transfer of knowhow in the semiconductor industry. But it also ran a persistent trade deficit. It did succeed in bringing Taiwanese public opinion round to seeing China as a bit less hostile, but at the same time the support for an indefinite status quo and thus indefinite autonomy only grew.

The Trade Tool Once More

Trade proved an important tool to strengthen relations with several other countries. China showed its most generous side, but in reality this generosity proved scant. The new generation mostly completed what Premier Zhu Rongji had set in motion. It was Zhu who masterminded the free trade schemes, partially in response to a feasibility study for a trade agreement between Japan and Singapore. Southeast Asia was his main focus. It is true that China sponsored various seminars that investigated options for trade liberalization in the ASEAN–China Joint Committee on Economic and Trade Cooperation throughout the 1990s, but it was only in 2000 that Zhu Rongji surprised his colleagues at the China–ASEAN Leadership Forum by proposing a full free trade agreement and the creation of an expert group to pave the way.[27] In 2001, Zhu almost personally initiated free trade negotiations with Hong Kong and Macao. Premier Wen Jiabao followed suit, approving preparations for new agreements with Australia, New Zealand, Pakistan, and Singapore. At a summit meeting of the Shanghai Cooperation Organization in September 2003, Wen proposed a free trade zone with the six member states, but Moscow politely declined. Wen was assisted in these talks by his able Vice-Premier Wu Yi and Commerce Minister Bo Xilai.

"Why did China make such an initiative?" Asia specialist Zhang Yunling asked with regard to the free trade agreement with ASEAN. "The answer lies in its growing confidence and the potential gains."[28] These gains in the first place related to market access for Chinese exporters. A simulation to which Zhang contributed predicted that a free trade agreement between China and the Southeast Asian grouping would increase China's exports by 55 percent and ASEAN's by 48 percent. Trade agreements were also expected to improve access to raw materials. Another reason for trade agreements was that they could enhance China's attractiveness as an investment market and a production hub for the entire region. At the same time, however, experts considered free trade agreements to be important instruments for competing with countries like Japan, South Korea, India and the United States. Several scholars depicted a situation in which regional powers were involved in a race for regional economic leadership, using trade agreements as the most important tool for gaining influence. Singapore National University's Zhang Xiaoji called this a contest for core status in Asian regional cooperation.[29] "The value chains resulting from the changes of industrial division of labor have not only brought closer economic relations, but also fiercer competition," he stressed.[30] Referring to the economic ambitions of Japan, India, and the United States, Hou Songling and Chi Diantang claimed that China wants to gain a foothold in a world economy with fierce competition. "If we cannot quickly make a major breakthrough in the FTA negotiations, some countries might shift their focus to possible FTAs with the United States," Zhang Yunling argued.[31]

Yet the omens for trade liberalization were not positive. In 2000 and 2001, news media brought an endless stream of stories about the disastrous impact of China's accession to the WTO on rice farmers, Thai shoe factories closing their doors because of Chinese dumping practices, China's textile flood, struggling cement producers in the Philippines, desperate electronic manufacturers in Malaysia, etc. This context of growing public pressure on Asian governments substantially raised the stakes for negotiating free trade pacts. But China found ways to reassure its interlocutors. First of all, it raised positive expectations. The most natural advantage was of course its burgeoning consumer market and Beijing went to great lengths to stimulate other countries' appetite for getting a chunk of it. "China's market is open and vast. The two-way trade is mutually beneficial," Bo Xilai assured.[32] More aid was granted and the debts of the poorest member states were waived.[33] For example, Indonesia was enticed with support for the development of telecommunications, agriculture, the reconstruction of tsunami-hit areas and hundreds of millions of preferential buyers credit. Vietnam was won over by supporting its bid for WTO membership and by pledging US$300 million in aid. Countries like Laos, Cambodia, and Myanmar received large amounts of aid via the Greater Mekong Sub-region.

During the talks, China also showed flexibility. The comprehensive economic agreement between ASEAN and China stipulated that the parties needed to "address their sensitive areas in the goods, services and investment sectors with such flexibility to be negotiated and mutually agreed based on the principle of reciprocity and mutual benefits." This left the option open for extending liberalization in other areas with individual countries.[34] Countries could bilaterally discuss with China what items were to be added to the sensitive list. Nations like Cambodia, Laos, Myanmar, and Vietnam got more time to reduce their tariffs and were allowed to have a longer sensitive list. Beijing also granted most-favored-nation status to Vietnam, Laos, and Cambodia. Even though these countries were not members of the WTO, this gesture gave them all trade advantages that any other nation received from the People's Republic. But China was not unique in this approach. India and Japan too differentiated between ASEAN member states. Japan managed to supplement its economic partnership agreement with seven bilateral free trade agreements that were more comprehensive.

What did distinguish the People's Republic from Japan and India in its negotiations was the ability of the central government to determine key national interests and to develop its policies accordingly. While lobby groups of farmers and trade unions hampered Tokyo, Seoul, and Delhi until the very final stages of their negotiations with ASEAN countries, Beijing followed a rather coherent agenda once its goals were set. This allowed China to make faster concessions in small but important niches, like fruits and rice, in order to make progress in larger economic sectors such as manufacturing. Thanks to this political leeway Beijing could pull a diplomatic masterstroke. It offered to phase out tariffs on selected agricultural goods like palm oil, timber and wood from ASEAN's six core members. This early harvest plan was presented as a boon for these countries' exports to China.[35] By incrementally acceding to demands for zero-tariff treatment on goods like fish, vegetables, and milk products, it succeeded in shifting attention away from competition in manufacturing to benefits in the agricultural sector. Neither Delhi, nor Tokyo or Seoul was able to offer such a package given their protectionist agricultural policies. The plan also sharpened the differences in interests among ASEAN member states. If countries added the same products to their early harvest basket, tariff corrections would apply for trade not only with China but also with the other countries. While countries like Thailand and Singapore requested an accelerated reduction of tariffs, others saw this as a threat to their agriculture and asked for additional protection. Hence, the early harvest scheme weakened resistance.

But even while many of its concessions looked generous, China managed to limit sacrifices. Take, for instance, the fact that Beijing agreed on a more informal trade regime, opposite to Japan's insistence on including very stringent rules beyond WTO standards in its trade agreements. The Chinese government considered that it was also in its own interest to settle disputes in a bilateral and informal way. With regard to the early harvest provisions, China had no interest whatsoever in restricting imports of agricultural goods from ASEAN. The contrary was true. The Chinese government had already started to implement tax cuts for the sake of food security, curbing inflation, and the development of a more competitive agribusiness. Moreover, it would have to apply many of the early harvest provisions automatically as a consequence of its WTO membership. None of China's competitors were able to emulate China's early harvest program as they all maintained the protection of the agricultural sector at the core of their trade policies. The Chinese government also did not expect that tariff concessions to ASEAN's poorest members would come at great cost. Vietnam would have received its most-favored-nation status automatically when it became a member of the WTO only two years after signing the agreement with China. Even the large amount of foreign aid that China provided was by no means as generous as its leaders pretended. Most of it consisted of export credit and loans, and needed thus to be paid back. In sum, the Chinese government was well aware that it depended on the political goodwill of other states. It therefore sought to negotiate smart agreements in which it weakened resistance by offering small concessions in a plurilateral way. China has proved that it can combine confidence, flexibility and charm to overcome distrust, to tie a vital region closer to its own market, and to stay ahead of its main competitors.

As regards the impact of the trade agreement, ASEAN gained, but China certainly gained more (see table 5.1).

Table 5.1 The evolution of exports between China and its partners (ASEAN, Pakistan, and New Zealand) after the trade agreements entered into force between 2010 and 2012 (in US$ billion)

	China	Partners
Agricultural goods	+3	+11
Ores and metals	+1	+2
Fuel	0	+6
Labor-intensive manufactured goods	+21	+3
Other manufactured goods	+46	+13
Total exports	+71	+34

Source: UNCTAD Stats

In the three years after the pact came into force, between 2010 and 2012, ASEAN's exports to China increased from US$113 billion to US$142 billion. China's exports to ASEAN surged from US$138 billion to US$204 billion. Out of the US$28 billion trade increase for ASEAN, US$6 billion consisted of fuels, US$5 billion of electronic components, US$4 billion of agricultural products, US$2 billion of ores, US$2 billion of chemical fertilizers, and another US$2 billion of basic plastics. ASEAN exports to China shrunk in the sectors of computers, electronic products, and steel. China gained heavily in manufacturing: US$22 billion in machinery, US$12 billion in textiles, and US$10 billion in steel. What China particularly achieved was to strengthen its position in labor-intensive products. ASEAN's exports of labor-intensive products were augmented by US$1 billion, China's by US$19 billion. "We are both markets with vast cohorts of people in need of jobs," an Indonesian diplomat lamented. "The current deal with China has only resulted in greater imbalances. Our trade deficit is up and our role is now even more limited to that of commodity supplier. That is detrimental to the long-term development and stability of the region."[36] The result of the agreement with Pakistan was similar. China's trade surplus increased and it made all the gains in advanced manufacturing. Pakistan's main interest in the trade deal was to increase its exports of textile yarns, which it did, but only very modestly. The increase in imports of yarn and textile fiber from China was as large as the increase in Pakistan's exports. The agreement with New Zealand resulted in a trade deficit, but the US$4 billion trade gain of the island state between 2008 and 2012 consisted almost entirely of meat and other agricultural products. It was different with Singapore. Singapore too turned a deficit into a small surplus, which consisted of 70 percent of manufactured goods, mostly advanced machinery. The Singapore deal revealed that China still had a way to go in strengthening its technological prowess, but altogether, the free trade deals with other Asian countries did permit

Beijing to fulfill its most important objectives: to create jobs for the Chinese masses and to get hold of raw materials. It did so with only very small sacrifices.

Rising Star

The first decade of the new century saw a surge in free trade multilateralism. China did not miss a single step. China's growth raced ahead, but that also meant that it could no longer stay quiet or, as Deng Xiaoping would have put it, keep a low profile. China's star was rising and so was its visibility. That visibility Beijing sought to take advantage of to highlight its peaceful and benign intentions. The Fourth Generation was largely successful in doing so. Even if it still did not make the slightest compromise on its main ambitions and the relations with many neighboring countries became increasingly unequal, it got away with it. It is difficult to assess how far this is to be attributed to diplomacy, the hundreds of official meetings, the innumerable conferences and fairs. There is ample evidence, as we will see in the next chapter, that the perceptions that most neighboring countries, their governments, and societies had of China did not became more favorable, that they did not believe in the diplomacy of peaceful rise, or assume that relations were indeed becoming more harmonious, or that China was truly interested in settling thorny disputes.

– 6 –

Elusive Harmony

President Hu Jintao read his last work report to the Party Congress in November 2012. He spent about 15 minutes explaining that China's diplomacy had changed profoundly. "A country should accommodate the legitimate concerns of others when pursuing its own interests and it should promote common development of all countries when advancing its own development," he said. "Countries should establish a new type of global development partnership that is more equitable and balanced, stick together in times of difficulty, both share rights and shoulder obligations, and boost the common interests of mankind." This statement reflects a first important transformation of China's policies towards Asia that we identified in the previous chapters: a growing recognition that its own development depends on the development of its large and needy neighborhood. This is not to say that early leaders were not aware of the importance of the prosperity of the neighborhood, but the more China became successful in its own rejuvenation, the more pressing the need for maintaining stability – at home and along the borders. It is hard to assess exactly how deeply these convictions are now entrenched in the mindset of decision makers. But I have no reason to doubt their sincerity when leaders like Hu Jintao highlight the need to strike a balance between China's interests and those of its neighbors. In informal discussions with Chinese officials, it always struck me how genuinely they believed that China was working for the common cause of Asia. Did China not create more economic opportunities? Did it not provide generous assistance? It is my conviction that many of those officials really came to recognize the *need* for regional solidarity and that they also came to believe earnestly that China *is* magnanimous. From their viewpoint, critics, like me, can only be mistaken or attempt to sow discord in Asia.

Policy Shifts

Those same officials would point to a second important policy shift: a growing willingness to show military restraint and to "shelve" territorial disputes. Whatever the accusations about assertiveness, the last military casualty was probably an Indian border guard who got lost in the mist somewhere in the late 1980s. From a Chinese perspective, that is a remarkable achievement, especially because many other powers are seen as bullies: the United States with its overwhelming capacity to strike, Japan with its plans to remove the pacifist constraints from its constitution, and India with its ambitions to turn the Indian Ocean into an Indian lake. Those perceptions matter: to most Chinese, it has become clear that fighting will come at a huge cost and imperil economic progress. But it is not about perceptions alone. China, for the time being, no longer has to fight to defend itself and that is primarily because its military capabilities are frightening enough. They deter other powers from the kind of interference and coercion that China had to fear during the Cold War.

This has allowed China to make another impressive achievement, that is, to secure a central position in the Asian economic order, but to use a very dynamic and comprehensive economic diplomacy to keep neighbors confident that they too would benefit from China's growth as long as they opened their markets to Chinese exporters and investors. Initially it wooed mainly Japan as an export market for capital goods, like machinery and construction materials. Subsequently, it presented itself as a cheap processing hub to investors from Japan, the United States, Taiwan, Singapore, and South Korea. Then, as its industrial boom accelerated, it approached the developing countries in Asia with promises to buy their raw materials and industrial components, preferably facilitated by free trade agreements. A while later, the Chinese government sought to cultivate economic expectations, by pledging large amounts of investment, in extractive industries, infrastructure, and low-end manufacturing. The next part of this economic charm offensive was to approach its neighbors as an important source of loans and other credit. The most recent evolution is to present China's burgeoning middle class as a future opportunity for all countries in Asia, especially those that have their eyes on jobs in manufacturing. The way the Chinese government has raised and cultivated economic expectations is intriguing, combining a clever use of skilled diplomats, lobbying from border provinces, high-level delegations, expert committees, business exchanges, loans, prestigious investment projects, and a gradual acceptance of regional cooperation. What a change this represents from the revolutionary prologue!

Regional cooperation leads us to another striking shift in China's policy toward Asia: its growing interest in multilateralism. For China, as for most other protagonists, multilateralism is the pursuit of power politics by different means. Multilateral organizations have benefited China in different ways. They gave the impression to groupings of small countries that they were at the center, and China used that confidence to overcome their reticence in bilateral talks. That was the case with the economic negotiations. As the neighborhood grew more concerned about China's competitiveness, China not only used the cover of regional organizations to approach countries one by one, it also tried to shape the new rules with those bodies to its own interest. When negotiations for a trade agreement with ASEAN were started in 2001, China's main offensive interest was to open its market for manufactured goods and it was rather reluctant to advance in services liberalization, as Singapore requested. But along the way, as China's services exports expanded, it became more eager to embed this sector in its economic pact with ASEAN as well.[1] As China's investments in ASEAN increased, it also became interested in a more advanced investment protection agreement. We could even apply this gradualism to regional financial and monetary cooperation: China only moved when its domestic economic situation was ready. Shaping the agenda and rules was also important in regard to security issues. China, for example, kept the members of ASEAN busy discussing maritime security, proposed several initiatives to curb piracy, and supported the region's combat against terrorism, but while that was happening it continued to increase its presence in the South China Sea and to resist any binding code whatsoever. Things were similar with the countries of the Shanghai Cooperation Organization. Beijing did not miss an opportunity to lead the quest for security against Islamic terrorism, but it declined any meaningful involvement of the Organization in issues of water security and the management of international rivers that were heavily exploited by China. In other words, regional organizations helped build confidence and keep smaller countries fixated with processes despite a lack of serious progress. The good thing, however, was that as long as regional organizations helped China advance its interests, a return to hard unilateralism could be avoided.

China has become more able to play the divisions between countries. It is clear that the Five Principles and the Three Worlds Theory of Mao Zedong were already first attempts to drive a wedge between the main powers and the rest, but that skill has only become more important. Consider the maritime axis between Japan and the United States, for example. Even if the two countries went further and further to stress their joint interest in deflecting Chinese unilateral action to change the situation in the East China Sea, Chinese spectators were well aware also that Washington did not want Tokyo to go too far in responding to alleged Chinese provocations or to change the status quo itself. Differences between Washington, Tokyo, Seoul, and Moscow also gave China more maneuverability in the Six-Party Talks and helped it avoid a complete stalemate between sanctions and Pyongyang's intransigence. Divisions between the ASEAN members permitted resistance in the South China Sea to be reduced. Similar maneuvering helped Beijing to advance its economic interests. The ASEAN–China Free Trade Area showcased how China used early harvest deals and other bilateral preferences to gain bargaining power. Even if it did not succeed in coaxing the countries of the Shanghai Cooperation Organization into a free trade agreement, it has played Kyrgyzstan, which as a member of the WTO must allow a free flow of goods, against the others. Obviously, China is not causing the divisions – these are the result of different geopolitical orientations and economic interests – but it has surely benefited from them.

The Security Environment

These five policy shifts are clear and irrefutable. It is this evolution that we could discern on the previous pages: the growing flexibility and adaptability of China's policy that prompted so many to argue that China is not a revisionist power, that it is thus not eager to reverse the Asian order, and that it does not seek to undermine the position of other powers. That, however, is premature. On the one hand, it was not just China that became more pragmatic. Asia has become more pragmatic too. It would be inadequate to identify the policy shifts on the Chinese side as the cause of the improving relations with Asia in the last decades. Throughout the previous chapters, we witnessed that the neighborhood often changed first. There was the diplomatic revolution of 1971, prepared by Henry Kissinger's secret diplomacy, with, in his wake, a throng of other countries that sought to normalize relations. While elections made governments oscillate between enthusiasm and fear about China, Japan tended to respond pragmatically to the political changes in Beijing throughout the Cold War. The collapse of the Soviet Union freed China of an important challenger. The economic conditions became better too. When Deng Xiaoping started his reforms, Japan had rounded the high-income cape of US$12,000 per capita and the United States showed more interest in investing in China as well. The search by developed countries for cheap labor proved especially helpful in offsetting tensions with Japan, the United States, and Taiwan. Then, after Japan plunged into stagnation in 1990, Southeast Asia was hit by the financial crisis of 1997 and 1998, and Lehman Brothers sent the United States into the worst recession in decades, the whole region was looking to China to come to the rescue. As China's economic growth took place in a more hospitable context, the slow modernization of China's armed forces took place in a security context that no longer threatened it like in the 1950s, 1960s, and early 1970s. The passage of American aircraft carriers, at the time of the crisis with Taiwan in 1995 and 1996, for instance, was hardly comparable with Washington's show of force in the Taiwan Strait in the 1950s.

On the other hand, we could observe that despite the changes in China's policy, it did not move an inch from its four great aspirations. First among them was the control over the frontier lands, regions like Yunnan, Tibet, Xinjiang, Inner Mongolia, and so forth. Throughout the previous decades, China has stubbornly resisted and sanctioned any attempt of other countries to interfere in these areas. It combined economic incentives with political repression to strengthen ties with the coastal heartland. It remains to be seen, however, how the growing unrest in Tibet and Xinjiang will play out in the future. Next came the ambition of the Party to be recognized and respected as a legitimate political structure. Economic success had made that task easier, but external criticism remains and internal impatience is growing as a result of economic difficulties, inequality, corruption, and pollution. China also had to be able to get its sovereignty respected: on paper through diplomatic recognition and in practice by resisting great power interference. That mission was also largely accomplished. The last and most contentious aspiration was to recover its lost territory: Taiwan, the islands in the South China Sea, a large part of the East China Sea, and a part of the disputed border with India. It is true that China settled other territorial disputes, but these were less important and the concessions that China made were small. In the remaining disputes, China has offered to invest with other claimants in economic projects, but it stubbornly refused to make any compromise. This aspiration to recover lost territory has damaged some of China's diplomatic achievements and, given the resolve of all claimants, risks to do more damage in the future. But there is no chance that China will backtrack from its claims. Even joint development presupposes that Beijing sooner or later expects to get its claims legally recognized and, at the very least, that it works towards effective dominance.

The repercussions of these aspirations also remain the same as 60 years ago. China has to maximize its power, to become the largest economy in Asia, and to build the most capable military force. That in turn implies that China will end the supremacy of the United States and tower above its neighbors as it did in the times of empire. Again, there is an important difference between this being the repercussions of static interests and it being a conscious

pursuit of officials. Most officials passionately deny hegemonic pretensions or a grand agenda to undermine other
powers. Most of them would recognize the desirability of
equality with the United States, the aim of recovering
lost territory, and that a rich China would mean a very
powerful China, but they are horrified at the prospect
of following the American example of unilateralism. I
find this a very important point to highlight. The main
cause of China's revisionism is not some sort of evil plot
among its officials and leaders. It is structural. As a result,
there is often friction between, on the one hand, the cooperative dispositions and values of officials and, on the
other, the inevitability of revisionism from China's inferior
position in the global order, its historical experiences,
its encounters with the power politics of others, and its
understandable great aspirations. That, on its own terms,
also explains a second friction, that is, the very manifest
friction between intransigence and flexibility in China's
foreign policy.

Maximizing power also does not necessarily equal territorial aggrandizement. As we have seen, the territorial
ambitions of China are limited to the recovery of *lost* territory. The legitimacy of these claims might be debated.
Many argue that China never owned the different places
and could thus also not have lost them. But the claims
and arguments cannot just be refuted and China also
has no plans, for the time being, to conquer *new* territory.
One could well imagine Beijing's ideal situation. The
area from Shanghai to Chengdu and from Shenyang
to Kunming would have turned into a high-income zone,
saturated with middle classes, and boasting advanced
industries, internationally renowned brands, and quality
services. Its main cities would specialize in different lucrative economies: Shanghai, for instance, in financial services, Chongqing in clean cars, Kunming in advanced
machinery, Chengdu in software, and so forth. Between
them, towns and villages would offer comfortable
and healthy living conditions in green garden estates.

Meanwhile, fast trains and airlines would channel millions of tourists and billions of spending to quiet places, to Tibet, emerging as the Chinese Pyrenees, to the Northeast, the future Chinese Alps, to Xinjiang, the new Andalusia, and to the southern beaches, China's Club Med. The China seas would be patrolled by a powerful Chinese navy, cheap workers from Vietnam would operate Chinese oil platforms, and Filipino waitresses serve Shandong Mary's or Beijing Bellini cocktails on new tropical resorts on the Spratly Islands. Taiwan would be a contented autonomous region of the People's Republic – oyster pancakes and bubble tea still being generously served.

The economy would be more efficient and thrive largely on domestic demand. That demand would gradually raise up the development of neighboring countries. China's new international champions would have tied them to the motherland by means of roads, railways, pipelines, and endless flows of visitors. They would control most of the production chain, from the mines to the retail chains, and trade mostly in Chinese currency. Russia's fate is obvious; Japan's would be comparable to a depopulating version of the United Kingdom, quietly musing on its great imperial past. Southeast Asia, China's Italy, would be vibrant and enthralling, yet heavily penetrated by Chinese companies, banks, and high-livers. The stretch from Bangladesh to Kazakhstan could well be China's Northern Africa and Middle East. Viewed from the Himalayan plains, it will undoubtedly emerge as a sweltering place. Having urbanized without industries, it struggles to bear its demographic burden and slithers from one political crisis to the next. India might turn into a loose confederation of competing states. As long as this instability can be contained and different governments played against one another, there is not much to fear. At the same time, a *modus vivendi* will have been developed with the United States, which allows China to establish de facto control over the disputed parts of its maritime margins and to turn Taiwan into another autonomous region, like Tibet and Xinjiang. In other words, the most effective form of revisionism would thrive on economic power politics, keeping military force as the feared tool of last resort.

In Defense of Peace

Becoming the most powerful country in Asia without having to fight for it and being constructive without having to compromise: that captures the way China approached its neighborhood. If one sets aside China's desire to maximize its power, it has been successful. Between 1990 and 2013, China's economy has grown on average by 10 percent per year, the rest of Asia by 5 percent. As a result, China's share in Asia's total output surged from 7 percent to 37 percent, which exceeds its share in the region's population. What mostly allowed China to outgrow its neighbors was its huge investment in infrastructure. Part of that flew to the manufacturing sector. Between 1990 and 2013, China's share in Asia's manufacturing output leapt from 9 percent to 47 percent. But this also became visible in other sectors: China's part in the total length of Asia's railways grew from 20 percent to 25 percent, its share in Asia's roads from 52 percent to 61 percent, its share in the number of Asian skyscrapers to 57 out of 74 buildings, its share in Asia's container port capacity from 32 percent to 51 percent.[2]

Those ports were important in supporting China's role as Asia's biggest trading nation. In 1990, China was still only the fourth largest exporter, after Japan, South Korea, and Singapore, but by 2013 its exports were larger than these other three countries combined. In particular its share in Asia's exports of manufactured goods went up: from 10 to 46 percent. Its part in Asia's exports of labor-intensive goods, important of course to keep the employment levels steady, even hit 51 percent. More important is

that China increasingly forced the other developing countries in Asia into the role of commodity supplier. China
also started to increase its share in advanced goods, like
semiconductors, cars, and machinery. More of these goods
were also produced by Chinese firms. If foreign investors
still generated 36 percent of Chinese industrial output in
2003, this figure dropped to 23 percent in 2013.

This growth caused a huge demand for raw materials
and China became the world's largest importer of most
commodities. Yet, between 1990 and 2013, China's permanent cropland doubled, thanks to new agricultural
schemes, giving it the largest farming potential only after
Indonesia. China's share of Asia's cereals production,
which is vital in terms of food security, remained steady
during this period at around 45 percent. This coincided
with soil degradation, but that has been a problem for
most Asian countries and China has been one of the few
to invest significantly in the fight against desertification
and fertilizer inefficiency. China's agricultural boom also
contributed to the depletion of freshwater reserves. In
comparison with Asia's average internal renewable water
reserves per capita, China faces scarcity. But compared to
other industrialized countries, China possesses significant
reserves of water, energy, and minerals. It is widely known
that the Chinese reserves of rare earths are vast and that
it controls much of other strategic deposits of precious
minerals. But thanks to recent surveying, it could also
expand its reserves of iron, copper, and bauxite. In terms
of energy, China boasts 60 percent of Asia's hydropower
potential and 25 percent of its coal reserves, but even its
gas and oil reserves are substantial – 5 and 11 percent of
Asia's total – and were expanded in the last two decades.
Its solar and wind power capacity represents 67 percent
of Asia's total. So, yes, China's need for natural resources
has increased, but its position is often better than that of
other important manufacturers, like Japan and South
Korea, and certainly more comfortable than the other
demographic giant, India.

Increased power has allowed China to make two other important achievements: to secure the support of its people and to obtain advantageous terms of trade with other countries. Surveys show that the economic confidence of Chinese citizens has grown from 52 percent at the beginning of the century to 82 percent and more in the last few years. This is significantly more than other countries, like the Philippines, Australia, Indonesia, Japan, South Korea, India, and Pakistan.[3] One important explanation is that China, together with Malaysia, is among the few Asian countries whose average GDP growth rates have remained above inflation rates. Between 1990 and 2013, Asia's average GDP per capita growth was 4 percent, but its average annual inflation rate was 9 percent. Much of the prosperity gains was thus leveled out by higher consumer prices. In China, though, the average GDP per capita growth was 9 percent, inflation only 5 percent. Chinese households also recorded the fastest increase in durable goods ownership.[4]

As regards the terms of trade, China ran an average trade surplus of 3 percent, whereas Asia as a whole ran a trade deficit. On the one hand, this helped China to acquire massive foreign exchange reserves, amounting to US$3.7 trillion in 2013, representing 51 percent of Asia's total reserves. It is true, indeed, that trade surpluses and foreign exchange reserves coincide with low consumption levels and that they usually imply large amounts of credit being provided to other countries, at the expense, again, of the domestic market. But that credit can also take the form of investment in strategic assets, like ports, mines, and oil wells, or be offered as export credit, which helps both Chinese manufacturers to gain market share and Chinese officials to gain influence. On the other hand, logically, it allowed China to steer clear of the high external debt levels that weigh on other Asian countries. In 2013, China's external debt equaled only 9 percent of its GDP, compared to the Asian average of 32 percent. The Southeast Asian countries, for instance, have external debt levels around 35 percent, and India around 21 percent, and they all failed to continue the downward debt trend that became manifest after the turn of the century.

Large gains in economic power bring influence, especially because they render other countries more dependent. Consider trade. In 1990, China purchased only 5 percent of the exports of its neighboring countries.[5] In 2013, this was 22 percent. To some markets, China became indispensable. In 2012, it took 89 percent of Mongolia's exports, 83 percent of North Korea's, 30 percent of Laos's, 26 percent of South Korea's, 19 percent of Japan's, and 18 percent of Kazakhstan's. In 1990, China represented about 1 percent of its neighbors' foreign investments.[6] In 2012, this was 12 percent. It had a very dominant position in Laos, with 59 percent, in Afghanistan with 32 percent, in Cambodia with 27 percent, and in Myanmar, Kyrgyzstan, and Tajikistan with 23 percent. Loans remain the most important source of China's economic power and influence. China does not report how much it lends to individual countries, but the total stock of its external loans and credit is vast: around US$165 billion in 2012. In this way China has become by far the largest lender in the region. In 2013, Japan, Asia's traditional banker, had a total stock of only US$83 billion of foreign credit.[7] Officials say that about half of China's foreign credit is lent to Asian countries, most of it in the form of export credit or concessional loans, tied to Chinese goods and services.

The gains in economic power gave way to important gains in military power. China's share in Asia's total defense budget increased from 4 percent in 1990 to 35 percent in 2013.[8] China's official defense expenditures are now by far the largest and are even bigger than what Japan, India, and South Korea spend together. That resulted first of all in larger investments in human resources. Soldiers get higher salaries, recruits better training, pilots more flying hours, sailors more days at sea, and so forth.[9] But it also allowed for larger investments in equipment. In 2013, China probably spent between US$56 and US$60 billion on military research, development, and acquisition.[10] At the beginning of the century, China relied entirely on imports for advanced weapons, but 13 years later it had indigenized the development and production of most important systems and, importantly, their subsystems, like engines, sensors, data-links, and missiles. In terms of hardware, China commissioned more fighter jets, navy ships, and military satellites than all its neighbors put together. As a result, China could dramatically increase its military presence along its border and in the adjacent seas. Today, its armed forces are able to raise the costs for its challengers enormously, probably enough even to gain the upper hand in short conflicts with Taiwan and with other neighbors over the South China Sea. Also important is that a large majority of the Chinese people support the use of military force to defend territorial claims. At times of war, China could also resort to large strategic reserves of energy and compensate for its long vulnerable supply lines through the Indian Ocean by tapping Central Asia or Russia. This all renders China's neighbors more than ever dependent on the military leadership of the United States and cooperation between Asian countries.

The balance of power has shifted in China's favor, but the countermoves of its neighbors have been limited. At the economic level, most of them have tried to secure business opportunities with China but also to limit its impact. Other developing countries attempted to protect their national champions by means of a more robust industrial policy. Some, like India, targeted China's alleged dumping practices by unilaterally imposing tariffs or by filing complaints with the WTO. Others, like Vietnam, South Korea, and Japan, sought to protect their exports by means of competitive devaluation. Also important was to stay ahead in the race for free trade agreements and to avoid more of the regional commercial flows being diverted to China. Raw materials producers welcomed Chinese investments, but limited those to minority positions, and worked harder to attract large mining companies from other parts of the world and to diversify their exports away from China. So hedging – avoiding the choice between resisting and serving a rising power, between balancing and jumping on the bandwagon – characterized the responses of most neighbors, not outright protectionism. The main objective was to profit from China, yet to avoid uncomfortable dependence and full exposure to its competitiveness. Initiatives like the Trans-Pacific Partnership already tilted toward balancing, as they clearly excluded China, but the feasibility of that partnership remains uncertain.

Hedging with a tendency toward balancing was also visible at the level of military affairs. On the one hand, governments supported more frequent exchanges with the People's Liberation Army and even limited cooperation in the combat against piracy and terrorism. On the other hand, however, neighbors responded to China's military might by investing more in their own armed forces. Japan prioritized the modernization of its navy and the defense of its southern islands. With China in mind, India upgraded its nuclear arsenal, increased its military presence along the Himalayan frontier, and increased its naval presence in the eastern part of the Indian Ocean. This coincided with the establishment of more military partnerships around China. Vietnam, the Philippines, and Japan became very active in this regard. Most of these partnerships were set up with other Asian countries, but by far the most significant outreach was to the United States. Whatever the strains and difficulties, the United States became more important than ever as a security guarantee against China's military rise.

Gaining Power without Resistance

Gaining power without creating too much resistance: that was the strategic window of opportunity that President Jiang Zemin had in mind. But China is not yet satisfied. First of all, China is not yet a rich country. In 2013, its national income per capita is US$5,910, whereas a rich country, according to the World Bank definition, must have an average income of US$12,000 or more. The very idea that China might become stuck in the middle-income trap is unthinkable to its leaders. There is one very compelling reason for this concern. If China were to get stuck at the current income level, it would imply almost inevitably that the economic inequality between coast and hinterland, cities and countryside, could not be reduced. As a result, one can only expect more social tension, political fragmentation, and problems for the Party's legitimacy. Moreover, much of its recent investment in infrastructure, real estate, factories, and office buildings is made to serve an affluent society, so if incomes did not rise many of these investments would turn out problematic, unprofitable, and even redundant. This is particularly worrisome, because most of these investments were made by turning trillions of dollars in household deposits into credit for governments and companies. It is not hard to imagine the consequences of a major bubble burst leading to loss of savings, especially when these savings are so important for a rapidly aging population.

China worries about external vulnerability as much as it does about internal inequality and instability. Even if the importance of foreign companies has diminished, China continues to rely on them for knowhow and access to overseas markets. The government, for example, still worries about the lack of strong Chinese brands, the weak position in technology-intensive industrial production, the relative weakness of commercial services, and the fact that large parts of the international supply chains are dominated by Western, Japanese, Taiwanese, or South Korean actors.

Nor is it satisfied with its military security. That becomes clear from its assessment of its environment. "There are signs of increasing hegemonism, power politics and neo-interventionism," the 2013 Defense White Paper stated. "Competition is intensifying in the international military field...China still faces multiple and complicated security threats and challenges...Some country has strengthened its Asia-Pacific military alliances, expanded its military presence in the region, and frequently makes the situation there tenser. On the issues concerning China's territorial sovereignty and maritime rights and interests, some neighboring countries are taking actions that complicate or exacerbate the situation." These concerns are not new, but that makes it even more remarkable. China's military modernization in the last decade has been unequaled and the balance of power has shifted in its favor. Yet, that was clearly not enough. An important weakness identified by the government is the lack of capabilities to engage challengers outside the second island chain, to project land forces over long distances, to stage long-range air force strikes, and to use outer space as a strategic advantage.

This brings us once again to one of the most sensitive parts of China's rise: the recovery of lost territory. The mutterings of American officials that the Senkaku islands are covered by the Treaty of Mutual Cooperation and Security and that the United States will thus have to support Japan in case of a conflict have convinced China that it should do more to deter its challengers. That was also the case with the South China Sea, another area where the United States clearly came to the rescue of smaller claimants, like the Philippines and Vietnam, even though it does not formally refute China's claims over most of the islands. "Washington does not say that we cannot claim the islands, but it has made clear that we cannot enforce our claims on the islands, so that still means that we cannot have them," an advisor at the International Department of the Communist Party explained. Taiwan also remained a concern. Beijing is well aware that the growing economic relations do not lead to more support for unification, but coincide with growing support for the status quo. From a Chinese viewpoint, this shows that the policy of carrots is not working and that Taiwan has not appreciated the mainland's generosity.

The Dilemma

So, here we arrive at a crucial juncture. The deep, implicit driver of China's Asia policy remains the maximization of power: power to control the frontier lands, to secure the position of the Party as the legitimate political government, to protect China's sovereignty, and to recover lost territory. That power maximization had to be pursued at the lowest cost, that is, without having to fight for it. In the last few decades, China has been remarkably successful in keeping its rise peaceful, thanks to the masterminding of a more effective policy, but also thanks to a hospitable environment. China was able to benefit from that context first by balancing between the superpowers, subsequently by cultivating the economic expectations, and, not least, because the prospect of a new regional order dominated by China, the shift from an America-dominated multipolar order to a China-dominated unipolar order, remained distant. In terms of economic influence, China's progress was spectacular and it certainly managed to profit more from globalization than its neighbors. Its role as an export market, investor, and lender became more prominent. Still, there was no neighboring country where Beijing was able to shape important sovereign decisions against their will. In other words, China's clout did not increase to such a degree that other countries had to fear for their sovereignty and thus to choose between competition and cooperation. The next two chapters investigate how China is evaluating this dilemma and how its efforts to maximize military and economic power are affected by it. Will it share more of its prosperity? Is it considering slowing down its military modernization?

– 7 –
Economic Power

Whenever they speak abroad, Chinese leaders like to emphasize that their country remains a developing country. They are right about that. An average Chinese citizen still earns about eight times less than a Singaporean or a Japanese. Yet, if we compare China with its wider neighborhood, it has clearly developed from a backward economy into an economy that elicits envy. Just consider its GDP. In 2000, it generated 14 percent of Asia's GDP with 37 percent of Asia's population.[1] In 2012, it represented 37 percent of Asia's GDP with 35 percent of its population. Yet this is the most modest change. Between 2000 and 2012, Asia on average saw its GDP per capita grow by 5 percent, China by 9 percent. China's asymmetric gains were even more obvious in trade. In 2000, China accounted for 12 percent of Asia's exports. By 2012, this had climbed to 36 percent. This still masks the fact that China especially consolidated its share in manufacturing. In 2012, it took 41 percent of the export of manufactured goods and 52 percent of the export of labor-intensive manufactured goods – these are indeed the kind of goods that developing countries need to trigger labor-intensive growth. Not surprisingly, this resulted in the rest of Asia being forced to play the role of raw materials supplier. In 2000, raw materials represented only 12 percent of the exports of China's neighbors. In 2012, this had grown to 25 percent.

On the Economic Battlefield

Economic success tends to become self-perpetuating, arousing the enthusiasm of foreign investors and allowing for more improvement in infrastructure, education, technological innovation, and so forth. In spite of rising wages, China retained its position as Asia's largest foreign investment destination – accounting for 35 percent of Asia's direct investment inflows in 2012. Between 2000 and 2012 China paved more roads than the rest of Asia put together. During that period, the number of internet subscribers per 100 people increased from 0 to 13, which is more than the Asian average and 10 times more than in IT-miracle India. Crucial also is the impact of economic success on the terms of trade. China ran significant trade surpluses with most of its neighbors. Once again, it became clear that if a new regional division of labor was materializing, China took most of the manufacturing and left raw materials to its neighbors. If one considers the increase in Asia's exports to China between 2000 and 2012, 53 percent of that consisted in raw material exports. In 2012, about 46 percent of Asia's exports to China was formed by raw materials.

This shift in economic power inevitably had an impact on China's political performance. To be sure, it has known growing unrest, but altogether, the Chinese government has performed relatively better in strengthening the confidence of its people. There are different ways to measure this. First of all, surveys of citizens' satisfaction with their country's direction show that at the turn of the new decade Chinese citizens are not only more confident, as we saw in the previous chapter, they are also much more satisfied: 85 percent, compared with 22 percent in South Korea, 24 percent in Japan, 35 percent in Indonesia, and

45 percent in both India and the Philippines. That in turn has led to growing dissatisfaction with the performance of governments in neighboring countries. Even before the devastating tsunami hit Japan in 2011, the failure to revive growth was rapidly undermining support for the government led by the Democratic Party. In 2013, a first government satisfaction poll in Vietnam showed how much parliamentarians loathed the economic performance of the government, to a degree even that the Politburo insisted that the poll should be canceled. In 2014, national elections in India punished the Congress Party for failing to address the country's economic woes and corruption. The weakening of support for national governments has made local politics more important, which traditional parties usually answered with more nationalism.

That nationalism was partially economic and partially Sinophobic. In Japan, Shinzo Abe won the elections, in the first place because of his sharp campaign against economic mismanagement by the Democrats and his promise to launch an aggressive strategy to shepherd the economy out of stagnation. Abe promised to make the country strong again. Most Japanese believed that this was urgent because of China's rise and not necessarily to challenge China's rise.[2] But the endless series of incidents between China and Japan made it easier for the nationalists to go beyond that mandate and to overcome the traditional divide between the prudent majority and the hawkish minority of frustrated youngsters, xenophobic middle classes, and the more patriotic older Japanese.[3] In Vietnam, the government has remained more reluctant but various new movements have taken the lead in propagating a more nationalist line toward China. The new politics of nationalism reflects deep grievances in Vietnamese society that result from a particular mixture of market reform and authoritarian politics, wrote Tuong Vu, which is fostering a new consensus for fundamental reform, political reform, and national rejuvenation.[4] The political elite cannot but follow. In India, political hardliners have always used the

China threat to blame governments for being weak and irresolute. The more these governments were plagued by economic problems, the more they tended to give in to such pressure and to act more assertively to prevent losing popular support. During the 2014 elections, the frontrunners Narendra Modi and Mayawati took the initiative in playing up the China threat, promising a bolder economic and defense policy.

Nationalism in Asia is a symptom of weakness, of economic uncertainty, and of the failure of politicians to meet the expectations of their people. Nationalism does not tackle these problems. It masks them, with some luck long enough to win an election. The problem with nationalism is that it creates an atmosphere of distrust. Even if it does not express willingness for confrontation with other countries, it does make it harder for elites to compromise, and that increases the chance of a confrontation after all. In Asia, the return of nationalism complicates China's rise. This is for two reasons. On the one hand, it shows that China's economic success is coming at a growing political cost. On the other hand, China itself thinks that it has not yet gone far enough in maximizing its economic power and that its neighbors have no reason to complain. So here is the crux of the issue: China is diverting economic opportunities from its neighbors, but it is not willing to make genuine compromises that remove the social breeding ground of Sinophobic nationalism.

This dilemma of China's economic rise becomes clear in the discourse of Chinese leaders. On the one hand, they assert, as Hu Jintao did in the previous chapter, that economic benefits have to be shared. "Economic development is the central task of China," Foreign Minister Yang Yiechi emphasized before the National People's Congress. "The focus of our diplomatic work should create a favorable international environment for the country, economic growth and also directly serve the economy."[5] Wu Jianmin, the former President of the China Foreign Affairs University, stated: "Economic diplomacy is becoming increasingly important and China should endeavor to create more common interests in its economic diplomacy. China needs to find mutually beneficial areas in handling economic and diplomatic relations with foreign countries."[6] On the other hand, though, officials continue to have a very suspicious attitude toward the economic environment. "China will face more competition from the developed countries and the developing countries. With the pressure of competitive integration in Asia, there is a risk of being marginalized. Nobody expects international governance to take a bigger role. The major developed countries have answered the crisis with reindustrialization strategies and the promotion of exports, while the major emerging economies also put more emphasis on the international market and try to attract foreign investment. In the next five years, consumption growth in the emerging markets will not make up for the slow growth in the developed countries," wrote a task force of the Development and Research Commission.[7] This has been echoed by senior leaders from the President to Ministers. All that has led them to assume that China has to work harder to stand on its own feet, to be more competitive, and to have its companies implanted favorably along the entire global production chain.[8] This chapter investigates this dilemma in light of China's industrial policy, its trade policy, its raw materials policy, and its effort to internationalize the renminbi.

A New Open-Door Policy

When the new leadership stepped into the spotlight in 2013, its main objective was to adjust China's development model so that the country could become rich and leap from US$6,071 per capita over the US$12,000 per capita threshold. To reach that goal, it vowed to work toward a gradual rebalancing from investment toward domestic consumption and from industrial production to services. This made neighboring governments hope that some of the Chinese industrial bustle would soon migrate to their needy markets. But that was not what Beijing expected. Rebalancing implied indeed that the relative importance of industrial production in the Chinese economy would diminish, but not that it would be allowed to decrease in absolute terms. The contrary was true. The new leaders quickly made new plans to strengthen the industry and to shift production from resource-intensive factories toward a production that was more intensive in terms of labor, capital, and technology. Even if it was aware of growing competition from other developing countries, China wanted more labor-intensive manufacturing, not less.[9] At the same time, however, it also sought to make a push in advanced niches with greater added value.

It is curious that several decades after the Great Leap Forward, Chinese politicians remained so fixated with industrial output. There are several reasons for this. First of all, officials reckon that China's industrial output per capita remains quite low and that it might have to double or triple again.[10] Second, investments in the industrial sector are believed to be vital to get China over the middle-income trap.[11] It is the industrial sector, after all, that is deemed the most powerful driver of technology and productivity gains. Third, a new wave of investments in advanced industries was seen as essential to lift China out of its inferior position in the global economic order and "to get a better position in the global division of labor."[12] Fourth, industrial power is considered the cornerstone of comprehensive national power.[13] Without strong, national industries, there can be no bargaining power against the developed powers and no prospect for military modernization. Premier Li Keqiang made that very clear: "Industrialization must be given primary importance as it is the driver of modernization." Ahead of the National People's Congress of 2014, Industry Minister Miao Wei was even more explicit: "If China wants to join the ranks of global economic powers, it must become an industrial powerhouse first," he said. "The industry has become the cornerstone of China's comprehensive national strength and increases its strategic capabilities to compete globally."[14]

The motivations behind China's industrial policy have thus not changed, but the policy itself has become more geared towards efficiency, innovation, and international competitiveness. In the coming decade, the Chinese government will thus not necessarily invest less in the industrial sector, but transfer those investments to factories that are more profitable and expose those companies more to the relentless competition of the open market. "We should strike a balance between the appropriate protection of infant industries and preventing these measures from blocking their ability to innovate and vested interests from blocking reform," clarified a senior official at the planning bureau.[15] In fact, China is set to become a catch-all economy. While it will consolidate at the bottom, and continue to compete with the labor-intensive industries of other developing countries, it has set its eyes on high-tech as well and is preparing for competition with countries like Japan and South Korea for semiconductors, advanced electronics, cars, biotech, and so forth. As a result, we can only expect that China's progress in production will continue to race ahead of its progress in domestic consumption. This new stage of industrial catching-up will thus render its industrial sector dependent on exports. China's surplus of trade in manufactured goods accounted for almost 11 percent of the sector's total output in 2012.[16] This was still only 3 percent in 2000.

Hence, China's push for industry will inevitably coincide with a push for exports. The government recognized this. In his report for the National People's Congress, Premier Li Keqiang spoke of a strategic priority to upgrade exports. The planning commission added: "We will consolidate our traditional advantages in export and stimulate the export of interrelated industries and services."[17] How would that be achieved? To begin with, China made plans to diversify exports away from the sclerotic markets in the West to other developing countries. To mitigate frustration about the consequent trade deficit, it would balance its exports of manufactured goods by more imports of raw materials. Second, Beijing promised more credit insurance and financing. In 2012, China already spent US$159 billion in export credit and US$161 billion in export tax rebates, implying that over 10 percent of its exports were covered by these forms of support. Third, it would make a greater effort to penetrate export markets and especially to expand its market share in developing countries.[18] Asia figures prominently in that export strategy. The region is reckoned to promise a huge commercial bonanza. It is a growing consumer market with demand for both low-end and high-end producers. It offers important opportunities to landlocked provinces. It is also seen as a natural testing ground for manufacturers to introduce new products, technology, and brands, a testing ground also where the presence of large Chinese communities can act as facilitators. But Asia is also a challenge. Chinese decision makers know very well that competition with firms from Japan and South Korea is ruthless and that there is a tilt towards protectionism. Asserted an official at the Ministry of Commerce: "The new trans-Pacific trade negotiations show us that we have to be part of our neighboring markets before they can close to us and divert trade away." That has led Beijing to push for more trade agreements, with South Korea, Japan, and Sri Lanka. In 2013, the government announced that it would also aim at more comprehensive deals and thus deeper liberalization. In spite of misgivings about the existing agreement, Li Keqiang proposed a liberalization upgrade to the ten ASEAN members. China has prepared dedicated export policies for machinery, pharmaceuticals, household appliances, IT, and so forth.[19] It continued to push for new physical outlets to neighboring markets: railways, roads, airports, ports, and so forth. Flagship projects like the Maritime Silk Road, the Bangladesh–China–India–Myanmar Economic

Corridor, and the China–Pakistan Economic Corridor all received generous support. Chinese firms were also given more encouragement to link up the factories at home with processing plants in the periphery. This was important to circumvent trade barriers, but also to entrench Chinese production networks more firmly in partner countries.

So, then, do China's neighbors have to worry about their economic future? If recent history has shown one thing, it is that China is able to reorient trade flows, once it has flagged an industry as strategic. Computer chips are a case in point. In the late 1990s, China stood nowhere, but after the government prioritized the sector, it emerged as the biggest Asian exporter after Singapore, elbowing Japan, the Philippines, and Thailand out of the market. Their exports shrank in absolute terms. The same happened in the solar industry, where Chinese exports crushed manufacturers in Japan and left the rest of Asia behind. It is obvious that the more complicated products get, the more fine-grained the specialization between markets becomes. If China, for instance, sets its sights on the next generation of clean cars, there could be endless opportunities for a large number of suppliers. Volumes matter, though. The domination of strategic industries usually has a large impact on international trade flows, especially when consumption in the home market lags behind. However it plays out, it is clear to China that the Asian battle for industry has only just begun. Using trade agreements, trade credit, and political persuasion, it will go all out to conduct its own kind of open-door policy and tie neighboring consumer markets firmly to its factories. This does not mean that China cannot take over the role of Japan as an important investor and job creator in the region, but for the near future China has no interest in such a spillover effect. That is also clearly reflected in China's outward investments. If we compare those investments with the total worth of the economy, the outward investment intensity of China was about the same as India's and less than half that of Japan and South Korea.[20]

Securing Raw Materials

In 1974, Deng Xiaoping focused his address to the General Assembly of the United Nations on raw materials. It was critical for industrializing countries, he argued, to secure the supply of raw materials and for other developing countries to prevent their precious commodities from keeping them in a position of inferiority. Strong countries, he said, have a tendency to take strategic raw materials and farming products, but to leave no opportunities for profits in manufacturing. Today, China has come to utilize its own raw materials as strategic assets. Like many other countries, it has restricted or discouraged exports and tried to harness its primary sector in support of its factories. Occasionally, this created a unique advantage, like with rare earth metals, which were absent in most other industrialized countries and could be sold at relatively low prices to Chinese producers of electronics, chips, and batteries. More often, however, the final advantages were less clear. Subsidizing iron ore or coal from relatively expensive mines to release it at low prices to the home market, for example, creates a competitive advantage for some exporting factories, but the cost is passed on to the government and, in the end, Chinese households.

For now, China goes on using its raw materials to support industrialization, whatever the ultimate financial and environmental cost for the society. This has been criticized by many of its neighbors. "We will keep pressing China on these unfair rare earths export restrictions," Japanese Trade Minister Yukio Edano said.[21] A second problem, which we have already encountered in previous chapters, is that China does what it used to criticize imperialist powers for: in its quest for industrial prowess, it forces other developing countries into a role of raw materials supplier. In 2000, 19 percent of China's imports from other Asian countries consisted of raw materials. In 2012, that was 31 percent. On a country-by-country basis, this division of labor is even sharper. In 2012, the median share of raw materials in Chinese imports was 71 percent, up from 58 percent. This pattern occurred not only in bilateral trade. In 2000, still 65 percent of the other Asian countries' exports consisted of manufactured goods. By 2012, this had dropped to 55 percent.

The division of labor between China and most of its neighbors is becoming sharper and sharper: China does the manufacturing and leaves the primary sector to others. But that is still not enough. China also wants to control a bigger part of the primary sector of its neighbors. In 2012, the Ministry of Commerce released a note that confirmed earlier plans to acquire strategic assets in the primary sector. Chinese companies primarily have to go abroad to export, the note instructs, but it also has to allow the country to secure the supply of energy, minerals, agricultural products, and marine resources.[22] The energy industry has been a longstanding target for the Chinese government. Even if not all the oil and gas produced abroad by companies is shipped back to China, it just strengthens those firms' international bargaining position. China's biggest success story in this regard is Kazakhstan, where 23 percent of the oil is exploited by Chinese enterprises.[23] Equity projects in Asia are particularly important because supply lines can be kept short. The targeting of the energy business was followed by the mining sector. Chinese mining companies have acquired strong positions in several Asian countries, like Mongolia, Myanmar, Afghanistan, Cambodia, and Laos.[24] China seems to be willing to follow the same path to Asian agricultural markets. The Ministry of Commerce traditionally includes farming as a priority in its investment files of other Asian countries, the Ministry of Agriculture is offering more financial support, and the State Council has flagged investment in foreign agricultural resources as a matter of great importance.[25] China has to follow the example of ADM, Cargill, Bunge, and Louis Dreyfus, argued Cheng Guoqiang, and to be strong along the entire value chain.[26]

This kind of resource nationalism has made other countries ask whether China could divert precious resources and upset the international market. Important in this regard is that the raw materials market has never been free, given the fact that governments in resource-rich countries control much of the extraction or at the very least who gets a concession for extraction. Furthermore, large multinational producers are often more dominant in setting prices than consumers. Some parts of the mining industry are undeniably dominated by an oligopoly of multinational firms. For most types of raw materials, China has not disturbed supplies to other Asian countries. China's share in Asian raw materials imports has grown phenomenally, but in absolute terms, the imports of other markets continued to grow too. There are two important differences, though. On the one hand, China drew more from its ores and energy from overseas sites owned by its companies. China has been very successful in acquiring mines and oil fields, thanks to its generous credit, and has often sidelined Indian, Korean, and Japanese competitors. On the other hand, Chinese imports of various commodities were remarkably cheaper. Compared to Japan and South Korea, two important net importers, imported natural gas was 55 percent cheaper, anthracite coal 53 percent, unrefined copper 34 percent, iron ore 53 percent, unwrought aluminum 46 percent, unrefined nickel 50 percent, and cobalt 46 percent. The quality of these imports, the concentration of ore and the purity of oil could explain a part of these price differences, but China's bargaining position certainly has had an important influence. Influence on raw material prices has certainly influenced China's industrial competitiveness, but not disturbed flows to other countries.

One good, however, has been an important exception: water. In comparison to Asia's average internal renewable water reserves per capita, China faces scarcity. But its 2,032 cubic meters per head is still much more than India's 1,149 cubic meters, Bangladesh's 689 cubic meters, or

Pakistan's 306 cubic meters. Even compared to Thailand and Vietnam, China's situation is not too dramatic. More important is that China literally sits on Asia's water tower. Almost all its water originates from domestic sources, like the Himalayas or the Tien Shan. India draws 25 percent of its water from international rivers; for Bangladesh, Pakistan, Thailand, Vietnam, Cambodia, and Laos, this is more than 50 percent. We all know that China is eager to build dams on these flows. In fact, most Asian countries are keen to tap the energy and water potential of these rivers, often rather recklessly, but China happens to control many of the headsprings and did not ratify many of the important guidelines such as the Convention on the Law of Non-Navigational Uses of International Watercourses. Beijing still considers the exploitation of its part of international rivers an internal affair.

It usually argues that its dams do not hold much water and that their reservoirs are small. This has been the case with the Mekong River for which China plans at least eight more dams. Whatever the plans of other riparian countries to develop their own hydropower projects, researchers agree that China's projects will have a large impact downstream. Chinese cascade dams could reduce the water level by 30 percent, reduce the fertile sediment by 55 to 94 percent, deplete fish stocks, and accelerate the regression of the coastline and saltwater intrusion. China has started to communicate more with its neighbors, sharing more information, and even exchanging experts on the matter, but its dam building plans were not held back by the many protests of environmental organizations, farmers, and politicians.[27] The same was true for the Salween, a long river that flows from Tibet to Myanmar. In 2006, Premier Wen Jiabao did suspend the plan for 13 dams out of environmental concerns, but in 2013 the project was restarted.

Even more sensitive is the Brahmaputra River, also originating in Tibet and vitally important to both India and Bangladesh. China has the blueprints ready for several hydropower projects on the upper reaches of the Brahma-putra, the Yarlung Tsangpo, and has started construction, yet claims that this will not reduce the volume of water flowing to the Indian subcontinent. In any case, Chinese officials try to reassure that most of the water flowing to India does not originate from the Tibetan glaciers, but from the monsoon rains that are discharged against the southern slopes of the Himalayas. What worries Dhaka and Delhi the most, however, is that China also developed several schemes to divert billions of cubic meters of water to the north. Beijing tried to talk down these fears, but there are plenty of indications that the plans for a major water diversion project are not yet off the table.[28] Already, one can see that all along the banks of the Yarlung Tsangpo, agricultural projects are expanding and modernizing.

But that is still modest compared with the agricultural boom along international rivers further to the west. From the southern slopes of the Tien Shan up to the border with Kazakhstan, irrigated fields with sunflowers, wheat, and rice reach as far as the eye can see. Through these meticulously ordered rectangles flows the Ili River. New canals carry its water up to 10 kilometers from its banks. Dams were built on its tributaries, like the Tekes and Kax Rivers. Two hundred kilometers further north, the same is happening along the Emil River. Irrigated fields and farms appear up to the Kazakh border. Beyond that there is only dry land. Another two hundred kilometers north flows the Irtysh. On its upper reaches, a large Haizikou dam reservoir emerges, followed by another dam at Fuyun, from where some first canals branch out. Fifty kilometers west, another dam with another canal apparently under construction. Forty kilometers west, one arrives at the Hinghe dam reservoir. From there a large canal was dug southwards to the Duhai reservoir, which in turn is the starting point for two other canals stretching hundreds of kilometers to Karamay and Urumqi. From Duhai also, smaller irrigation canals radiate in all different directions, supplying a stretch of farmlands of at least 300 square kilometers. Satellite maps also show that this irrigation network continues to expand. Recent plans of the Xinjiang regional government put a lot of emphasis on water conservation and more efficient irrigation, but Xinjiang's draft plan for economic and social development of 2014 still includes several new dams, at least one other water diversion project, and more ambitious goals for agricultural output. In 2013, approval was also given for another dam on the River Tekes and related irrigation facilities.

Important is that Kazakhstan depends on these rivers for about half of its renewable water supply. Research has shown that the discharge of international rivers like the Ili and the Irtysh has been falling for many years and that there is a risk of the country's large lakes shrinking. Meanwhile, the Chinese government has been doing what it usually does in such situations: talking without making concessions. In 2001, it agreed to establish a joint river commission with Kazakhstan, but limited its mandate to monitoring. In 2011, an agreement was signed on water quality protection and the China–Kazakhstan Friendship Joint Water Diversion Project on the Khorgos River, but no commitments were made to share the water of the Ili and the Irtysh equally.

It is interesting to observe that China expects to keep resources for itself, while it expects as much access as possible to resources abroad. This goes particularly for the global commons. Consider the high seas. China regulates the economic use of its exclusive economic zone strictly, but pushes for a very liberal regime in the oceans. As China has been depleting fish stocks in its adjacent waters, it encourages its fishing companies to venture into distant waters, like the Pacific Ocean and the Indian Ocean. Even if its fleet still tends to be primitive, it has the largest distant water fishing capacity in the world. Still, it has not ratified the agreement on compliance in vessel licensing or the fish stock agreement. It is also reluctant to give the Food and Agriculture Organization a strong mandate to monitor fish catch. The Chinese government also wants a flexible regime to exploit the floor of the oceans. It has invested a lot in special vessels for research, successfully applied to the International Seabed Authority to search for minerals in the Indian Ocean and the Pacific, and is now developing various new platforms to exploit them.[29] The main target is a wide array of minerals like cobalt and manganese, as well as rare earths and hydrocarbons. China, however, also expects to extract methane hydrate or combustible ice. This is a natural gas enclosed in crystals that can be found in large quantities underneath the ocean floor. In the Arctic and Antarctica as well, the Chinese government insists on freedom of exploitation. It rejected Australian, European, and American proposals to establish a marine sanctuary spanning 1.6 million square kilometers of the Ross Sea. It remains reluctant to accept Western proposals to prohibit fishing in the Arctic Ocean now that it is becoming more navigable. It is equally lukewarm about extending the moratorium on mining in Antarctica that is due to expire in 2041. China's quest to take its share of the global commons is backed at the highest level. President Xi Jinping has underscored the practical importance of ocean and polar resources.[30] "It is necessary for us to fully understand the resources on the continent," says Guo Peiqing, a professor of law and politics at the Ocean University of China. "China's exploration is like playing chess. It's important to have a position in the global game. We don't know when play will happen, but it's necessary to have a foothold."[31]

Internationalization of the Yuan

A third dimension of China's economic ambitions concerns its influence on the regional financial order. China has clearly taken a leading role in Asia's search for more financial cooperation. In the Chiang Mai Initiative, essentially a large pool of foreign exchange reserves from which members can draw in times of severe financial problems,

China emerged as one of the two largest contributors, alongside Japan. But the resources of the Initiative remain small. In the last decade, China came to wield more influence by offering bilateral loans to neighboring countries. In the 1990s, it waived the debt of several of Asia's poorest countries, like Laos, Cambodia, and Mongolia. After the Asian Financial Crisis it also stepped up its aid and investment. But that generosity is limited. Chinese loans have become much larger, compared with in the 1990s, and China now insists much more on debt being serviced. It also refrained from responding to requests from Pakistan in 2008 to provide several billion US dollars of financial support, so that Islamabad in the end had to approach the International Monetary Fund.

More importantly, there is the role of the yuan. The more countries used the yuan as a reserve currency, the more that would reflect China's economic power. In theory, major reserve currencies reflect the confidence of other countries in the strength of the home economies. In practice, a major reserve currency often reflects the importance of that economy as a consumer market for the rest of the world. That position as a central consumer market usually entails deficits on the current account, and it is exactly by paying more to other countries for imports of goods and services than it earns from exporting goods and services that its currency starts to circulate more widely. There used to be a time that each new bill had to be matched by a certain amount of gold in the treasury, but as that is no longer the case, a reserve currency becomes a reflection of strength and weakness at the same time. It is a reflection of weakness because when other countries pile up large reserves of the currency it often means that they are providing credit to consume. The long-term disadvantage is that it encourages overconsumption and external debt, which will lead to painful adjustments. The short-term advantage, however, is that countries with reserve currencies can print money without causing inflation. Having most of the trade in your own currency usually implies smaller transaction costs. If, on top, commodity markets run on that currency, exchange rate fluctuations will have a much smaller impact on the price of imported oil, ores, and so forth.

So, the main concern with the internationalization of the yuan is that it could finish the so-called privilege of countries like Japan and especially the United States to maintain their high standard of living by having others buy their currency or different sorts of debt denominated in their currency. If the yuan were to become an attractive alternative to the yen and the dollar, it could impel those countries into a painful adjustment crisis. Many experts have argued that a yuan block in Asia is in the making. It is not the case, yet. In 2013, the share of the yuan in official foreign exchange reserves and in the security stocks of banking industries remained smaller than 1 percent.[32] This is normal because the yuan cannot be internationalized on a large enough scale as long as China runs a current account deficit. The yuan is thus not yet close to an important role as a reserve currency. But it is becoming a reference currency. The fluctuations of Asian currencies are found to be closer to those of the yuan than to those of the dollar and the yen. That is normal, because Asian economies have come to depend more on the Chinese economy as an export market or deliberately tried to avoid their currencies appreciating too much in comparison to the Chinese yuan. The difference from a reserve currency, however, is that a reference currency does not enable Beijing to get much direct benefit from it.

The only gain, for now, is that more trade transactions are settled in yuan. In 2013, more trade deals were financed in yuan than in yen. That, as indicated before, helps China to become less affected by the fluctuations of the dollar. This could become particularly important in the energy and mineral markets. In 2012, for example, China for the first time signed some large oil and gas contracts in yuan instead of dollars. Some of this trade is facilitated by currency swap agreements by which the Chinese central bank swaps an amount of yuan for an amount of the other currency to finance bilateral trade. Large currency swap agreements were signed with South Korea, Hong Kong, Malaysia, Indonesia, and so forth. Yet again this is not enough to turn the yuan into a reserve currency, because most of the Chinese currency ends up back in China through trade. For now, China does not even want to turn the yuan into a reserve currency.[33] "We never think about whether the renminbi will become a reserve currency of other countries," Liu Mingkang, former head of the China Banking Regulatory Commission and President of Bank of China, said. "We can never put the cart before the horse... Comprehensive renminbi international and capital account liberalization should be the last step of financial sector reform."[34]

Only in the long run is there a chance that the yuan will challenge the position of the yen and the dollar. Ten to twenty years from now, China's financial sector could be mature enough to handle a more volatile in- and outflow of capital. By then, the government could also have become confident enough about the competitiveness of its industries, and that competitiveness could have helped China get into the league of rich societies, having a per capita GDP higher than US$12,000. At that point, there would no longer be a need for large exports of industrial goods. Domestic consumption could be promoted and even some current account deficits tolerated. That instantly brings us to the crux of the debate about a potential leading international role of the yuan: China needs to be a strong, leading economy first. That is not yet the case, and the leaders in Beijing know it. If China continues to rise economically, one could even ask whether it is that important for the yuan to become a reserve currency. It would already entail that the United States and certainly Japan had lost their dominant position. Losing the reserve currency would only be an additional insult and make it harder for their people to adjust to the new reality. The United States might offset some of that because shale gas will allow it to spend less on imports, but Japan does not have that luxury and would almost certainly be absorbed in a new Sinocentric economic order.

Risk of Setbacks

Will China keep its growth on track so that it can become a high-income country? The Chinese government will do everything in its might to make that happen. However much has been written about rebalancing toward more domestic consumption, Beijing believes that it should first make its industries more competitive and boost its productivity. It is this transition from a middle-income country toward a high-income country that will be particularly challenging. There are three reasons for this. For the Chinese government, this will be a period of great nervousness as long as there is even the slightest chance of getting stuck in the middle-income trap. China cannot settle for the position of a middle-income country. "That would mean that the social gaps will remain, that the economy will still be vulnerable, that we cannot build prosperous cities, that the Party's future is put at risk, and that China will not be influential in international politics." From that perspective, any setback also becomes a threat to the four great aspirations. That risk of setbacks will be significant. Even if the introduction of more market mechanisms can allocate investments more efficiently, China has a tendency to transfer vast amounts of household savings, about US$4.5 trillion in 2013, to investments in the industrial sector that are not viable without export, investments in public infrastructure that count too much on future demand, and investments in risky real estate. In other words, the gap between investments and the actual demand in the Chinese domestic market will become larger and, given the problematic organization of debt markets, stock markets, and public finances, this could lead more easily to crises. The main risk in that regard is not so much that

China as a whole is too heavily indebted; the main risk is that Beijing's economic strategies have transferred too much household savings to risky projects and nothing is more risky for the survival of a government than to put the savings of industrious families at risk. There is another reason to watch this transition period cautiously. To become a rich economy, China will count on exports to develop its industrial base. Beijing does plan to partially offset those exports by imports of raw materials, but other Asian economies will find it very hard to maintain or develop their own manufacturing sector and to diversify their exports away from raw materials. This could lead to more frictions and more distrust with regard to China's rise.

– 8 –

The Contest for the Pacific

One of the repercussions of China's four great aspirations is that it has to become Asia's most potent military player and to be able to keep the United States at bay. This is especially important in light of the objective to recover lost territory – Taiwan, most of the China Seas, and some stretches of Himalayan mountains. This is turning Asia into the new frontline of an astounding tussle in which the United States tries to maintain its military dominance and China seeks to end it. One can expect this to lead to a new strategic equilibrium. Some countries could seek security by moving closer to the United States and balance against China, while others might opt for moving closer to China and to bandwagon. This would not end competition and uncertainty, but at least create a situation in which the smaller players get enough security insurances and the two protagonists can go on almost indefinitely in a military tit-for-tat. This new conflict formation bears resemblances to the Cold War. But this is unlikely for three reasons. First of all, the large Asian countries are not as battered and obedient as most of the powers were after World War II. Japan, India, Russia, and Vietnam will resist being turned into the pawns of a chess game that takes place above their heads between Beijing and Washington. Second, the conflict concentrates not so much on sharp boundaries and diffuse proxy wars, but on fluid and highly politicized borders. Third, the climax of tensions is unlikely to coincide with a period of economic growth and optimism as impressive as at the outset of the previous Cold War. Instead, the time of Asia's easy growth will probably come to an end and give way to economic uncertainty and political nationalism.

Reuniting the Motherland

In its endeavor to recover lost territory, China has started to change the economic and military status quo. Whether it concerns the East China Sea, Taiwan, the South China Sea, or the disputed border with India, it has enlarged its economic footprint and started to alter the military balance of power. It did not, however, change the political and territorial status quo. That bothers China. In the previous decades, China consistently combined proposals to shelve territorial disputes with efforts to show its resolve. Even when the whole world came to perceive it as assertive, it never allowed tensions to escalate. This was for a combination of reasons: it was not provoked by major unilateral changes of the territorial status quo, it was not ready to impose its interests through force, and an escalation of tension was not deemed to be as rewarding to the elites in Beijing as the successful pursuit of growth. That does not mean, though, that the value of those disputed territories diminished or that the Chinese government has come to fret less about possible unilateral alterations in the status quo. It implies even less that it has given up on recovering these pieces of lost territory. What is more, Beijing has more frequently emphasized that any obstruction to this aspiration will impel China from its trajectory of peaceful rise.

This was made very clear to Japan. In the East China Sea, as we have seen, China has rapidly altered the economic and military status quo, and expected Japan to learn to live with that. Tensions had been building after a Chinese fishing boat rammed two Japanese coastguard ships, Chinese ships consequently started to patrol the area, and the governor of Tokyo decided to buy the Senkaku or Diaoyu islands. When the Japanese government sought to prevent the patriotic governor from acquiring them, it decided to buy the Senkaku or Diaoyu islands itself from their private owners in 2012. Beijing denounced this as theft, stepped up its surveillance missions around the islands, and initiated one initiative after the other to assert its claims. It established an air defense and identification zone that went well beyond the Japanese median line and covered the disputed islands. It expanded gas-drilling projects in the Huangyan field, about 25 kilometers from the Japanese median line. Chinese coastguard ships were deployed for the first time near the disputed islands. Since the nationalization of the islands and the election of the nationalist President Shinzo Abe, relations with China have never recovered. In April 2014, after a year of growing tensions, senior officials from the International Department of the Communist Party and the Foreign Affairs Office of the Central Committee explained that China would not back down and that it was up to Japan to adjust.[1] Qian Lihua, one of the more vocal Chinese generals, echoed: "At present we cannot completely rule out the possibility of clashes in East Asia, but it is not decided by China." Experts believe that Japan is only at the start of a rapid military modernization and that the United States will do nothing to stop that. Furthermore, they also argued that economic reforms in Japan were a failure and that this would lead to more nationalism.[2] Chinese and Japanese surveys from 2012 found a large majority of Chinese respondents to be willing to defend the islands, even by force, and that a small majority thinks armed conflict likely.[3]

Then there is Taiwan. The more China invested in closer relations, the more the Taiwanese wanted to keep it at a distance and the less supportive of reunification they became. In the public domain, Chinese officials and experts tend to be prudent in commenting on this development. Most of the academic assessments of the evolving cross-straits relations since the election of President Ma Ying-jeou in 2008 are positive.[4] Analysts have also argued that the nationalist party, the DPP, has become more constructive and learned to appreciate the fact that the Taiwanese economy cannot afford a collision course with the mainland.[5] The Sunflower Protests in the spring of 2014 were mostly described by Chinese commentators as an expression of Taiwan's idle youth and its ailing democratic system. Occasionally, however, decision makers did signal that closer relations were not enough. On the sidelines of an APEC summit, in October 2013, President Xi Jinping conveyed to a senior Taiwanese politician that exchanges soon had to move beyond commerce. "Looking further ahead, the issue of political disagreements that exist between the two sides must reach a final resolution, step by step, and these issues cannot be passed on from generation to generation," he said.[6] A few weeks later, this was confirmed by the State Council's Taiwan Affairs Office: "Like it or not, the political agenda exists objectively. We need to face it sooner or later. We can start with economics and then politics, but we can't go by economics alone and no politics at all."[7] Informally, officials acknowledge that it would become very difficult for the Chinese government to refrain from sanctions if a new nationalist government were to replace the Kuomintang and halt or reverse some of the cooperation, or just destroy the prospect of a satisfactory political reunification. Meanwhile, the government reports that 94 percent of the people insist on a rapid reunification of the motherland.

In regard to the South China Sea, the Fifth Generation of leaders showed no inclination to relinquish the nine-dashed line, but officials and experts seemed to work toward an interpretation that was more defensible in the framework of the International Convention of the Law of the Sea. It implied, among other things, that China would delimit its exclusive economic zone around inhabitable islands and only territorial waters around the smaller islets. This way, China could still administer most of the South China Sea. Moreover, if a 200-mile zone were drawn around, for instance, Woody Island in the Paracel archipelago, and Fiery Cross Reef in the Spratly Group, the two zones would overlap in the center of the South China Sea, so that China could also administer all transit between the islands and, according to its understanding of the law of the sea, ban foreign military presence. The difference from the East China Sea is still that these disputes are less sensitive. Initiatives of Vietnam and the Philippines to defend their interests are annoying, but not as antagonizing as the posturing of Japan. One Chinese official put it: "If Vietnam were to change the territorial status quo unilaterally, we would teach them a lesson, but not go to war. With Japan and Taiwan, this is different."[8] China is concerned, however, about the interference of external powers, like, again, Japan, but also the United States, India, and Australia. A majority of the Chinese people seems to be approving of the use of force to recover disputed territory.[9]

Decades of growth have not brought China an inch closer to the fulfillment of one of its four great aspirations. That leaves an uncertain future in which the territorial status quo can be challenged in different ways: by changing the reality on the ground, as a unilateral political decision of China, as a unilateral political decision of one of its neighbors, or when an incident spirals out of control. "On the issues concerning China's territorial sovereignty and maritime rights and interests, some neighboring countries are taking actions that complicate or exacerbate the situation and Japan is making trouble over the issue of the Diaoyu Islands," the 2013 Defense White paper summarized. This uncertainty is one of the most important drivers of China's military modernization. It can only reunify the motherland or prevent others from snapping up bits of disputed territory if it develops a strong military that can overwhelm its neighbors, independently, in an alliance, and in a formation with the United States. In this endeavor, it seems to be supported by the Chinese people. A large survey in different Chinese provinces in 2014 revealed that 92 percent of the respondents worried about the country's "complex security environment" and that 73 percent supported a "substantial increase in military spending."[10]

An Unsatisfied Giant

Gone is the time of mocking China's floating junkyards and flying scrapheaps. Even if the People's Liberation Army still trails far behind the United States, its recent military modernization is impressive. As a result, Asia has come to worry much more about China as a military threat. This has manifested itself in three important ways. To begin with, political leaders simply made plain in official statements and documents their apprehension of China's alleged military assertiveness, their unease about its growing presence in disputed areas, and their frustration about the lack of transparency in China's military modernization. Second, neighboring countries became more determined to weave a web of security partnerships around China. At least 19 new defense agreements were signed between 2009 and 2011, the period when concerns about China's alleged military assertiveness peaked. Vietnam became the spider in this new web of partnerships. Hanoi negotiated ten new military cooperation schemes, followed by Japan and South Korea, which signed five such documents each. Most of these new plans were centered on maritime security and several were accompanied by statements of concern about the tensions in the South China Sea. Some, such as those involving Vietnam and the one between Japan and South Korea, were path-breaking, although it has to be said that this agreement was mostly related to North Korea and that all other documents involving South Korea were mostly related to cooperation between defense industries and trade in defense systems. Highlighting this evolution even more was the fact that Indonesia was the only country that concluded a defense agreement with China during this period. A third trend was that neighboring governments went further in straining their budgets to finance new military hardware: submarines, fighter jets, drones, and so forth. Defense budgets peaked in absolute terms. Yet, even as a share of GDP, official expenditure went up in Vietnam, South Korea, and India.[11]

This did not go unnoticed in Beijing. The tone of the Chinese government about the military power politics in the Pacific has become more negative. President Xi Jinping asserted that the "tendency towards hegemonism, power politics, and new interventionism" had increased.[12] The 2013 Defense White Paper was particularly critical. "Some country has strengthened its Asia-Pacific military alliances, expanded its military presence in the region, and frequently makes the situation there tenser," it observed. An interesting sounding board of the strategic debates in China's capital is the selection of papers of the International Department of the Communist Party from contributions to *Contemporary World*, a journal that it publishes bimonthly, alongside the shorter comments of experts in outlets like *Xinhua*. Since 2011, the annual assessments of the security environment in *Contemporary World* have become more skeptical. While its authors maintained that the trend towards peaceful cooperation has survived, they signaled that the Asian order had become more complex and volatile.[13] "The arena of great power rivalry is shifting from the Atlantic to the Pacific," summarized Zhang Xuanxing of the Central Compilation and Translation Bureau.[14] The main concern throughout the papers was Japan's more muscular behavior. "Of all the major powers the fiercest rivalry is with Japan," the Central Party School's Zuo Fengrong concluded.[15] Concern was also expressed about America's tendency to encourage resistance among smaller countries. "China's neighborhood is a very fragile and complex geopolitical area," Tsinghua University's Zhao Jin wrote in a lengthy paper. "China feels itself increasingly squeezed... Because of growing asymmetry, there will be more competition with neighboring countries, which will be seized as an opportunity by global powers to infiltrate, stiffen China's attitude, and make neighboring countries even more resolute to pit China against extra-territorial powers."[16] Tao Wenzhao, a senior researcher at the China Academy of Social Sciences, warned that the United States risks emboldening Japan in the East China Sea dispute.[17]

When the Chinese government and its advisors state that their country has become the target of new hegemonic policies, their worries are genuine. The whole world has been echoing the complaints of Japan and the United States that China is seeking to deny access to its adjacent seas, while a formidable screen of sensors and steel is pulled up all along the first island chain around China. If China is pursuing an area denial strategy, the reasoning goes, the United States and its partners are pursuing an ocean denial strategy.[18] Beijing not only finds this situation threatening. It also finds it very unfair that the United States is claiming the moral high ground as the magnanimous lord of the waves and portraying China as the greedy oppressor of the Asian seas. From a Chinese viewpoint, it was the United States that started to throw its military weight around more assertively and to send surveillance ships right up to China's territorial waters at the end of the 1990s. It is America's interpretation of the law of the sea that is prob-lematic. It is America that wickedly assumes exclusive economic zones to be freely accessible to foreign navies and seeks to corner China by pushing for international arbitration, even if it knows that it can never bring a solution for most of the disputed islands. It is America also that pretends to be generous in sharing the Pacific Ocean with others, even tauntingly inviting the Chinese navy to patrol around Hawaii, while it goes all out to maintain its naval supremacy. America is taking advantage of the natural anxiety that coincides with China's rise and the many territorial disputes to uphold its global maritime hegemony, to contain China's naval ambitions, and to prevent it from fulfilling some of its core ambitions. Many of these frustrations are warranted. China and the United States are locked into a geopolitical dilemma. It is about two sides trying to gain security in the Pacific by maximizing their military power. The United States tries to keep its defense perimeter as close to Asia as possible; China tries as hard as it can to break through it. But the United States has cleverly turned it into a political dilemma and even a moral dilemma between China and the rest.

That leads to a dilemma similar to that in economic affairs: to back down or not to back down? It is clear that China wants to attenuate tensions by investing more in diplomacy. But there is no chance that it will slow down its military modernization. "The US is currently planning to deploy three carrier combat groups in the western Pacific region. If this deployment becomes routine it will constitute a major threat to eastern China, and will allow US forces to closely monitor all activities of the Chinese navy in the western Pacific," writes Han Xudong, a professor at the National Defense University.[19] "It was the US that disturbed the military balance in the western Pacific region," he continued provocatively, "so it is the US that has to halt its military maneuvers to help slow the developing regional arms race." As that is not going to happen either, we can only expect China to try harder to swing the balance of power back to its advantage. President Xi Jinping seems even more devoted than his predecessors to modernizing China's armed forces and to readying it for larger missions beyond China's borders.

American Primacy in the Pacific

This new effort to strengthen China's capacity to defend its maritime margins means essentially that it has to undo the current situation in which its military capabilities within the first island chain are vulnerable to strikes from the first island chain or from submarines, aircraft, and carriers that lurk a bit further in the Western Pacific. That will be a huge task, as China well understands, because the United States is taking the lead in a series of military modernization initiatives that could harm China's position within the first island chain and prevent it from moving beyond.[20] "As America believes that the Dong Feng 21D anti-ship ballistic missile is the biggest potential threat faced by the US Navy since World War II," claimed *People's Daily*, "it is being forced now to make the necessary changes to uphold its military superiority."[21] A much-quoted article in *Military Digest* argued that America's Air-Sea Battle concept is seeking to prevent the emergence of a Chinese defensive perimeter 600 kilometers from its shores.[22] The Air-Sea Battle concept has been widely discussed. Chinese experts reckoned that it would consist of several important changes: even more emphasis on air superiority, more unmanned vehicles, a better integration of space systems, the integration of air, sea, and undersea warfare, the improvement and integration of intelligence, better surveillance and reconnaissance, offensive information warfare, the use of new warheads, the development of hypersonic weapons, and so forth.[23] One commentator considered this all a new "sword of Damocles" dangling over China's future.[24]

Chinese experts have followed closely how Japan and the United States invested in their capacity to monitor possible threats from missiles and aircraft. Japan traditionally maintains a dense chain of FPS-3 and seven-story-high FPS-5 radars that can monitor most of the East China Sea. This network has been upgraded and strengthened by two powerful American FBX radars in the north of the country and near Tokyo. Japan and the United States have a permanent fleet of 13 destroyers with potent Aegis radars in the area.[25] Japan plans to expand its capacity by at least two more destroyers. Japan also continues to modernize its four E-767 Airborne Warning and Control Planes (AWACS). All these detection systems require vast processing capacity. Without computers and control rooms to oversee the theater, detection is of no use. In that regard as well, Japan and the United States are investing in more speed, reliability, and coordination. At least as important are the capabilities to monitor the Chinese navy. The large fleet of American and Japanese P-3 maritime patrol aircraft has been partially replaced and partially strengthened by an even more potent fleet of ten Japanese P-1 and six American P-8 planes.[26] The P-8 is by far the most potent naval patrol aircraft ever built and a powerful weapon against Chinese submarines. It can drop both sonobuoys and missiles to engage submarines and surface combatants and features very fast and precise data processing systems. A navy version of the Global Hawk, the MQ-4C Triton (BAMS), will assist in these patrol duties.

In the last decade, the United States has intensively deployed Towed Array Sensor Systems in the East and South China Sea to map the area for anti-submarine warfare.[27] This also explains the frequent encounters of small, unarmed surveillance vessels like the USS Bowditch and the USS Impeccable with Chinese ships. The next step is to ready a series of potent detection systems. The United States continues to modernize its Fixed Distributed System (FDS). That system consists of a large number of small, interlinked floating passive sensors that can intercept the noise of passing submarines and reconstruct their path. A new project, the Reliable Acoustic Path System (TRAPS), is also made up of many passive sonars. But they sit on the seafloor and are wirelessly connected to a floating surface node, whose signals can be picked up by planes, ships, etc. Recently, a surface node, the Expeditionary Autonomous

Power Buoy (LEAP), was completed. The buoy can be powered by tidal energy, is thus permanent, and has a much greater capacity to process signals. The TRAPS system will likely be linked to a new system, the so-called SHARK, an unmanned underwater vehicle designed to track submarines and, probably, to be equipped with a warhead. This system would be useful mostly to monitor Chinese submarines within the first island chain and along the sea lanes that give way to the Pacific.[28] For the Pacific Ocean itself, the United States uses its sound surveillance system and is preparing an unmanned deep-sea sonar system (the Bluefin) that seems to anticipate the next generation of Chinese nuclear submarines. *People's Daily* asserted that the United States aims at a three-dimensional system to combat Chinese submarines, including a fixed underwater array system in key sea lanes like the Luzon Strait and the straits formed by the Ryukyu Islands, satellite reconnaissance and aerial reconnaissance, and a coordinated use of navy vessels like the Virginia-class attack submarines, destroyers, and littoral combat ships.[29]

Besides this shield of sensors, China looks up at a formidable wall of plate steel and missiles. The rebalancing of the American navy started well before the Obama administration explicated its pivot to East Asia in 2012. Already in 2001, Submarine Squadron Fifteen was reactivated at Guam. A third submarine joined the two initial nuclear attack submarines in 2004. The Destroyer Squadron 15, homeported in Yokosuka, was expanded as well. If the Squadron included four large surface combatants in 2001, it now has seven Arleigh Burke-class destroyers and two Ticonderoga-class cruisers. In 2005, the United States decided to homeport the USS Washington in Yokosuka, the first nuclear powered aircraft carrier to become permanently based overseas. It arrived in 2008. Meanwhile, three more mine countermeasure ships were homeported in Sasebo and six new ACU-5 landing craft arrived. Littoral combat ships were positioned in Singapore. Altogether, the United States usually has about 34 destroyers,

17 nuclear attack submarines, and two aircraft carriers in the region. In the coming years, the capacity will be enhanced by a new generation of more survivable long-range anti-ship missiles (LARSM), new Triple Target Terminator supersonic air-to-air missiles. "The LARSM is meant to engage rivals like China when GPS guidance is disturbed," writes the *People's Daily*, "It will have an extraordinary range, precision, and the ability to carry out deadly attacks in any combat environment. The signal is clear: do not intimidate our great white fleet. It implies that the Chinese navy now has to spend many more years catching up with the US Navy."[30]

Japan's fleet was not just modernized; it is also expanding.[31] Japan has purchased four large helicopter carriers, much bigger than the ones built in the 1990s. The number of conventional attack submarines is expected to grow from 17 to 22. It will also enlarge its destroyer fleet with at least two new air defense destroyers. Chinese observers have also noticed new capabilities to guard the disputed islands. "A MV-22 that takes off from Futenma base in Okinawa needs just 60 minutes to reach the Diaoyu Islands and it only needs 30 minutes if it takes off from Miyako-jima," posited one article. "A Global Hawk that takes off from Okinawa can fly over 30 hours over the Diaoyu Islands and detect almost everything up to the coastline of the Chinese mainland. So, if Japan imports more than three Global Hawk unmanned aerial vehicles, it means that it can have uninterrupted aerial surveillance over the Diaoyu islands."[32] Du Wenlong, a military affairs commentator, added that Japan was investing in a "chain of land-based anti-ship missiles" that could deter China from sailing through the sea lanes to the Pacific Ocean.

China has also noticed new developments in space. "Space is well integrated into the Air-Sea Battle strategy," posited a Professor at the National Defense University.[33] Since 2001, the National Reconnaissance Office has launched five satellites for naval reconnaissance and signals intelligence gathering. Between 2001 and 2013, at least 25 other satellites were put into orbit for electronic intelligence, radar imaging, optical imaging, and optical reconnaissance. During the Cold War, naval space-based radars were used to track warships and to detect air defense systems. In 2011 and 2012, the National Reconnaissance Office had a record four launches per year. In 2013, the Department of Defense (DOD) said: "We are developing options to counter the space capabilities of potential adversaries."[34] The DOD is investing in several programs to increase its capacity to detect and track very small objects in space. What also attracted China's attention was the Prompt Global Strike Program. To reduce its dependence on overseas bases and airspaces, the United States is working on a new medium-range tactical ballistic missile that can be launched from a submarine, and a hypersonic strike missile.[35] Chinese observers have taken a great interest in the X-37, a reusable unmanned spacecraft. "It can carry out reconnaissance and surveillance tasks, but it can also be equipped with missiles, lasers, and other advanced weapons against enemy satellites, and even to attack enemy ground targets."[36] A researcher added that to make the Air-Sea Battle concept work, the US must strive towards space command.[37] Chinese news media and experts have also taken a great interest in the latest Quadrennial Defense Review, issued in March 2014, and its emphasis on "space control."[38]

Chinese Countermoves

From the Sea of Japan to the Great Australian Bight, China watches itself being surrounded by an intimidating shield of plate steel, sensors, and missiles. Chinese experts are unanimous: China can have no coastal defense, no chance to recover its lost territory, and no security for its economic heartland without deterrence in the Western Pacific. Proclaimed Mei Wen, the first Political Commissar of the Liaoning Aircraft Carrier: "Whether it is the first island chain or the second island chain, the development of our navy should not be bound by chains but take distant oceans as its beacon."[39] An expert at the Naval Military Academic Research Institute added that hyping China's efforts to "break through island chains" testifies to Cold War thinking and should "not shake the resolve of the Chinese military."[40] "We need to have some security space. That is a general law for big powers," writes Ren Weidong, one of the more outspoken researchers of the China Institutes of Contemporary International Relations. "To achieve a new equilibrium in the Asia-Pacific, we must enhance our military presence both in the territorial waters and the Western Pacific. China does not seek hegemony, but it must attain some sort of military superiority in the region so that none of its opponents can prevail."[41] Cao Weidong, a researcher of the Naval Military Studies Research Institute, said that increasing China's military presence in the Western Pacific is critical to creating strategic depth. "Under the conditions of modern warfare, it is impossible to implement active defense with small and medium-sized vessels in the coastal waters alone."[42] Experts also refer to the need to increase China's maritime defense depth.[43] "To maintain sovereignty over the South China Sea, for example, we must develop naval and air facilities on Hainan and other large islands," one officer wrote. "Yet, because of the lack of a clear perimeter, those facilities are vulnerable to repression from the ocean. To reduce that threat we have to enhance our offshore defense capabilities."[44] All these arguments are often made by referring to the endorsements of previous leaders – from Mao to Hu – for the creation of an ocean-going or a blue water navy.[45]

So what does this mean in practice? It is not clear and unlikely that there exists a single strategy. Yet, several policy vectors can be distinguished. First of all, China continues to draw clear red lines and to show resolve in territorial disputes. The new generation of leaders has made it crystal clear that it would not tolerate unilateral changes to the territorial status quo by its neighbors. Second, it continues to diversify the options for escalation management – deploying more ships and planes of constabulary agencies – and centralize decision making in a Central Leading Small Group on the Protection of Maritime Interests that was established in 2012 and in the recently founded National Security Council. In 2013, many of the constabulary tasks were centralized around the newly established coastguard, which was to hit a staff level of 16,000 officers and to receive dozens of large patrol vessels, several with a tonnage larger than a frigate. It did not take long before these vessels were dispatched to disputed waters. Third, it will go on to try to defuse resistance by engaging in dialogues, military exchanges, and probably proposing more cooperation in the exploitation of adjacent seas and soft security issues. Fourth, there is a persistent tendency to divide resistance by exploiting different interests among the Southeast Asian countries, by tirelessly reminding the rest of Asia of the threat of Japanese militarism, by keeping Russia on its side, and portraying the United States as an unreliable and selfish hegemonic power. But the main goal remains to alter the military balance and to challenge America's predominance in the Western Pacific.

This means in the first place that China will establish its permanent military presence in the Western Pacific.[46] President Xi made it very clear in a personal meeting with President Barack Obama that the time of America's domination of the Pacific was drawing to an end: "The vast Pacific Ocean has enough space for the two countries, China and the United States."[47] Military officers speak in this regard about the normalization of the navy's and the air force's presence in and above the Western Pacific waters. "This is perfectly in line with international law," insists Geng Yansheng. "China enjoys the freedom of passage and overflight."[48] The 2008 Defense White Paper highlighted the aspiration of the Navy to "improve in an all-round way its capabilities of integrated offshore operations." This was reaffirmed in the 2013 edition:

> The Chinese Navy is to improve the training mode of task force formation in blue water. It organizes the training of different formations of combined task forces composed of new types of destroyers, frigates, ocean-going replenishment ships and ship-borne helicopters. It is increasing its research and training on tasks in complex battlefield environments, highlighting the training of remote early warning, comprehensive control, open sea interception, long-range raid, anti-submarine warfare and vessel protection at distant sea. The PLAN organizes relevant coastal forces to carry out live force-on-force training for air defense, anti-submarine, anti-mine, anti-terrorism, anti-piracy, coastal defense, and island and reef sabotage raids. Since 2007, the PLAN has conducted training in the distant waters of the Western Pacific involving over 90 ships in nearly 20 batches. During the training, the PLAN took effective measures to respond to foreign close-in reconnaissance and illegal interference activities by military ships and aircraft.

These priorities are nothing new, but they are emphasized much more than in the past.

There remains disagreement about whether the development of a blue water navy primarily serves a mercantilist or Mahanian strategy that aims at protecting commercial lifelines, or a strategy of deterrence that seeks to keep enemies out of the Western Pacific. It is probably a combination of both, but offshore defense through a blue water deterrence capability seems to be key. To begin with, China is preparing larger and more frequent maneuvers in the Western Pacific. The so-called Mobile V Exercise in November 2013 was a first showcase of deploying different fleets in unscripted distant three-dimensional naval combat simulations.[49] Second, offshore defense remains the main justification for important new weapons systems. Modern aircraft battle groups, flanked by major surface combatants and nuclear attack submarines, generate expeditionary capacity but also serve as a deterrent to other large fleets.[50] China is planning to deploy at least four aircraft carriers. Its next carriers will almost certainly be larger than the Liaoning and have a flat top. They will likely be equipped with electromagnetic catapults, which have a positive influence on the energy efficiency of the ship and the lifetime of the planes, and a whole new range of advanced command and control systems.[51] Meanwhile China continues to work on the development of its J-15 carrier-based multirole fighters and has made some first steps in the development of an unmanned aerial combat vehicle, the Lijian, that might operate from an aircraft carrier. Research on the supply of carriers shows that Chinese experts see it big: they would be embedded in a large escort group and be able to operate in distant waters for a long time.[52] That escort group will thus consist, among others, of new nuclear attack submarines. The T-093 submarines, which have been operational since 2009, are largely considered to be no match for the American and Japanese navies. As a result, only a few were built and used mostly as a test bed for reducing their acoustic signature, sonars, precision-guided maneuvering torpedoes, torpedoes that can be used against other torpedoes, and so forth.[53] Research again shows that there are high hopes for the next generation of nuclear attack submarines, the T-095. It has to be quicker and more potent in terms of command and control. Papers show that China has invested in various research programs related to quiet magnetohydrodynamic propulsion, torpedo defense, and noise-reducing hulls. The escort groups would also include a new generation of guided missile destroyers, the T-052D, which features more advanced sensors and missiles. In 2013 alone, four of these new destroyers were launched. Pictures were also released of what is probably a program for a new cruiser.

Meanwhile, China is set to continue to strengthen its defenses in closer waters. China seems to be pursuing a swarming strategy. It is commissioning a very large number of mostly small platforms with a limited reach, which makes it risky for high-value platforms to enter China's maritime periphery. This starts with a dense network of sensors. China traditionally deploys many mobile coast-based types of radar, but has also started to test a new maritime patrol aircraft, based on the Y-8, and anti-submarine warfare aircraft. These planes will probably have an operational range of 1,500 kilometers. But China is also building its own network of undersea sensors. The Chinese navy is reported to have experimented with disposable sonar buoys. Academic publications show a lot of research on networks of undersea sonars and *Xinhua* published a long article on it in early 2013.[54] It appears that three acoustic monitoring centers are linked up to different underwater fiber-optic detection networks.[55] That all has to support an expanding fleet of warships, consisting of more than 50 T-022 missile ships, the new T-056 corvettes, of which at least 19 had been launched by early 2014, and a few dozen modern conventional submarines. Old fighter jets are being rapidly replaced by fourth generation J-10 and J-15 variants, which can be equipped with potent anti-ship missiles.

China is also trying to play its part in that contested interface between earth and space – also called *linjin kongjian* or near space.[56] Between 2006 and 2014, China launched at least 19 remote sensing satellites or satellite combinations. Article abstracts in prestigious reviews like the *Journal of Astronautics* show that the scope of research is vast. China is clearly working toward more advanced optical, radar, and electronic intelligence satellites to monitor its naval frontier and to track missiles.[57] "Ocean surveillance satellites are crucial…throughout recent wars, long-range precision strikes from large surface combatants have become decisive and to deal with them we need to improve our naval remote detection capability."[58] It invests in the maneuverability and survivability of those platforms.[59] It is known to have several experimental maneuverable satellites in orbit, which should be able to evade attacks, but also to attack other satellites. Following the example of the United States and Russia, it acquired missiles and lasers that can be used against satellites. In 2014, it became the third country to test a hypersonic glide vehicle, the WU-14, which is a very fast, maneuverable warhead that can be an even more potent threat and penetrate the defenses of aircraft carriers that lurk in the distance.[60] Also in the wake of the United States, China is testing its own unmanned space plane, the Shenlong.[61]

Littoral Balancers

China and the United States are set for yet another arms race, one that will mainly manifest itself in the Western Pacific, in space, and in cyber. The options for a military tit-for-tat-without-victory look endless – at least as long as economic resources are plentiful. One could expect this to lead to a bipolar formation in which China faces up to a grand alliance of littoral balancers led by the United States. Japan would be in that alliance, the Philippines, Australia, Vietnam, and probably also India. What most of these countries have in common is territorial disputes with China, a legacy of tensions, and enough strength to clench a fist. This would deter China from altering the territorial status quo unilaterally or from using force to advance its interests. In other words, basic security would be guaranteed and that could pave the way for confidence building, measures to avoid miscalculations, and sustained economic relations.

Even if basic security could be guaranteed, the possibility of a bipolar regional order still imposes on the regional powers the choice between resisting China and learning to live in its shadow. Shadow implies an unpleasant loss of status, greater difficulties in protecting important interests, and also in obtaining advantageous terms in bilateral exchanges. It is thus about prestige, power, and prosperity. The prospect of an existence in the shadow of another power should be no reason to fight, as long as it does not presage eclipse. That is, at least for the first decade or so, something that a grand alliance around the United States could prevent. It will be hard, though, to build such formation. Asian powers are hesitant to throw their lot in with the United States. True, Washington has worked hard to reaffirm its role as a strategic partner. Japanese perceptions of the United States have also improved. So did Vietnamese and Korean perceptions. Indian perceptions, though, remain much less positive. Polls reveal that only a minority of Indians are positive about the United States. More important than perceptions is the fear of excessive dependence. Delhi has a clear policy of diversifying its strategic partnerships and pursuing indigenous military modernization. It has been happy to receive American support, but is loath to get too close. The same goes for Vietnam. For both domestic political reasons and strategic calculations, it continues to balance its partnership with the United States with closer cooperation with Russia. Japan has been seeking to complement its maturing military ties with Washington with a normalization of its own capabilities and to rebalance the trans-Pacific security ties. If such normalization is already sensitive in the light of Japan's imperialist history, the eventual nuclearizing of Japan's armed forces is even more so.[62]

But if the Asian powers do not want to depend too much on the United States, would it not be enough to strengthen relations among themselves? Matching strong bilateral partnerships with the United States with strong Asian partnerships would permit an even stronger coalition. Consider Australia and Japan, for example. Since 2013, an Australian frigate is homeported in Yokosuka, next to American navy ships. Or take India and Vietnam. Since 2013, India has been training Vietnamese submarine sailors. Another example is Japan's delivery of two patrol boats to the Philippines in 2014 to strengthen Manila's capability to patrol the South China Sea. These synergies certainly matter, but they are by no means substantial enough to offset the concerns that emanate from the unequal partnerships with the United States.

In this context it will thus be difficult to develop a grand alliance that balances against China in a measured and coordinated manner. This will be complicated by another factor: nationalism. There are of course many forms of nationalism, but three characteristics are common. First, Asia is not a bunch of battered states, which Europe was when the United States spearheaded the transatlantic alliance against the Soviets in the 1950s. Most Asian states are young, restless, fixated with status, and ambitious to advance their own interests. Second, nationalism is strengthened by domestic and international uncertainty. It explains the electoral victory of Shinzo Abe in Japan, of Park Geun-hye in South Korea, and of Narendra Modi in India. Third, as seen in the previous chapter, Asia's new nationalism is increasingly Sinophobic. Abe and Modi have all made reference to China's rise in order to urge for programs of national rejuvenation, industrial development, and military modernization. In Vietnam, the government encourages public media to report on frictions with China in the South China Sea and even started to celebrate the historic battle with China over the disputed Paracel Islands. This Sinophobic nationalism also comes from the grassroots. Whether from textbooks and propaganda or not, student movements have been protesting China all over Asia, with the Sunflower Movement in Taiwan as an interesting new phenomenon.

That leads us back to another observation from the previous chapter: Asia's new nationalism is partially a symptom of its growing socioeconomic troubles and those problems are likely to increase. We are thus likely to enter a period in which more mutual concessions are required to ward off more dangerous confrontations, but in which politicians also will be less willing to make such concessions. The fundamental dilemma remains that between China's great aspirations and the expectations of its neighbors. As with its economic rise, China has also ventured to the awkward point where other countries start to have serious concerns about its military power, but it thinks itself that much more effort needs to be made to gain military clout. That produces a host of secondary dilemmas, security dilemmas mostly, but also territorial dilemmas. Particularly worrying here is that even if the territorial situation remains unchanged, the reality on the ground – the presence of warships, the activities of oil companies, and the role of coastguards to enforce sovereignty claims – does change and makes incidents more likely, incidents with politicians pressured to stand strong, incidents also with a greater risk of spiraling out of control.

— 9 —

Another Great Power Tragedy

China presented its rise as a paradigm shift, an alteration not so much of the balance of power, but of the very guiding principles of international politics. This book has demonstrated that it is not a paradigm shift, at least not to the degree that it will overcome the fretful and violent tensions that have coincided with rising great powers in the past. This does not refute the general observation and feeling that China's policy toward Asia has changed, become more sophisticated, and shown more flexibility. In the period between the proclamation of the People's Republic and the trumpeting of Xi Jinping's China Dream, we could clearly discern how China successfully developed policies that prevented its neighborhood, that long belt of uncertainty, from turning into a geopolitical straitjacket. The correction after the Cultural Revolution was spectacular, not only the diplomatic revolution of 1972, cautiously concocted by Henry Kissinger and Zhou Enlai, but even more so Beijing's skillful normalizing of relations with its neighbors. We saw Deng Xiaoping offering preferential trade, recommencing trade with South Korea discreetly via Hong Kong, proposing joint energy development with Japan in the East China Sea, suggesting a gentlemen's agreement to Vietnam, starting border talks with India, and testing the waters in multilateral organizations, even if that implied that Taiwan could retain its membership as an economic entity.

Policy Changes...

Under the leadership of Jiang Zemin and Hu Jintao, that diplomatic offensive gained momentum. China not only joined more regional organizations, it also became more active in shaping their agenda, and set up its own regional initiatives. It signed one investment agreement after the other and initialed its first free trade schemes. It masterfully turned the Asian financial crisis into an opportunity to build trust and advance its prestige. Land border disputes with several countries were settled and the armed forces were instructed to start exchanges with most neighboring countries. China's diplomacy toward Asia morphed from a rigid state-guided scheme into an eclectic array of initiatives from many stakeholders: the state, the Party, the military, the provinces, cities, companies, think tanks, and so forth. Even when China became more frequently accused of assertiveness and tensions built up in its maritime periphery, it sought to mitigate fears. Although there seldom was progress on the substance, it made sure that the process of dialogue continued. New working groups were set up with the Southeast Asian countries to follow up on the declaration on the code of conduct on the South China Sea, and the Treaty of Amity and Cooperation was signed. With Japan, it negotiated a memorandum on the development of the East China Sea and with India it initialed a roadmap to facilitate border negotiations.

The official discourse developed accordingly. Clearly, Chinese leaders saw the downside of their country's resurrection at the geographic center of Asia from the beginning, hence the promises of Mao that he would steer clear of the path of hegemony. No leader formulated this more unambiguously than Deng Xiaoping. If one day China should change her color and turn into a superpower, subject others to her bullying, aggression and exploitation, he said, the people of the world should oppose it and overthrow it. Hence, the promise of a peaceful rise. In the 1950s that reassurance took the form of the five principles of peaceful coexistence. The emphasis was on sovereignty and non-interference. Between the 1970s and 1990s, this narrative was complemented with a glorification of the economic benefits, first by highlighting China's role as an investment market, then by stressing the prospects of a mutually beneficial division of labor. Later on, the focus shifted to China's growing importance as a financial stabilizer, an emerging consumer market, and a large investor. With the new security concept of 1995, Beijing vowed military restraint and cooperation with its neighbors to tackle common security challenges. The policy of peaceful rise made more or less the same promise in different terms.

Policy changed, discourses changed, and, I venture to conclude, even the state of mind changed. It is of course very difficult to measure how deeply Chinese participants in the relations with neighboring countries have been socialized with the norms of cooperation, open trade, and peace. It also goes beyond the scope of this book to provide an accurate assessment, but it is obvious that many Chinese today think differently about international politics than the generation that experienced both the civil war and the revolutionary stage. Struggle no longer dominates. It is a combination of struggle and cooperative opportunities that characterizes contemporary Chinese reflection. My personal experience with Chinese officials and experts, responsible for Asian affairs, is that they truly seem to believe that the only chance for China to become a rich and stable country is to rise peacefully and that concessions toward its neighbors are inevitable. That does not mean that they resign from their duty to advance the national interest, but that national interest has, from their viewpoint, become more aligned with the interest of Asia as a whole. Of course, this leaves questions. Diplomats are supposed to keep relations steady and many Chinese experts are expected to resonate the official message of peace. These are thus the people supposed to be nice, but behind them is a vast cohort of decision makers who have much less opportunity to get familiar with the complexities of China's neighborhood and are also much less interested in making sacrifices for the sake of stability. So, we could infer, socialization has started in a small cosmopolitan group, but still has to trickle down quite a bit if the new values are to permeate the whole of Chinese society. In other words, there has been socialization of the cosmopolitan few, but not of the state as such. That is also exactly what Chinese diplomats recognize themselves. As one official put it: "The rest of our government is quite inward-looking and is only just starting to understand the diplomatic consequences of our success."[1]

...and Policy Inertia

That instantly leads us to perhaps the most important argument of this book: for all the policy changes, China's interests have changed remarkably little. The first chapter identified them as the four great aspirations: the integration of frontier lands, to keep the people supportive of the Party, to get sovereignty recognized and respected, and to recover lost bits of territory. The first three have become less pronounced, largely because China has been successful in fulfilling them. But there can be no mistake: throughout the previous decades, each attempt to interfere with the frontier lands, especially Tibet and Xinjiang, was sanctioned resolutely. Political visits were canceled, investment projects put on ice, and containers of food left rotting in Chinese ports. Whenever the role of the Party was questioned abroad, Chinese officials angrily left meetings, often freezing exchanges for weeks, months, and longer. But, equally so, China responded anxiously to each external challenge to the economic progress that underpinned the Party's popularity. Australian mining companies will never forget how they were pressured; Southeast Asian countries look back with very muted feelings on the way Chinese officials played them in the run-up to the free trade agreement. In pursuit of diplomatic recognition and sovereignty, China went all out to charm and pressure countries to turn away from Taiwan. It only decelerated a bit after President Ma was elected, at the point that the row of flags in the main hall of the Taiwanese Ministry of Foreign Affairs had shrunk from over 70 to 21. The last aspiration remained the most challenging one. The recovery of Taiwan, the islands in the China Seas, and a part of contested Sino-Indian borderland remains, for now, a pipe dream. Nevertheless, China continues to sanction unilateral attempts to change the territorial status quo mercilessly, intercepting trawlers, sending warships to contested waters, and almost theatrically trying to starve a lonely group of Filipino guards, as their stranded ship gets slowly consumed by the salty water of the South China Sea.

Is this greed? Are these four great aspirations part of a callous plot to enslave the rest of Asia? Are they, as neo-classical realists surmise, an expression of the authoritarian politics of the Communist Party? This book has asserted that the answer to all three questions is no. The first chapter showed how many of these aspirations were the result of a long, humiliating exposure to the bullying and the blackmailing of the two superpowers. The consequent sense of insecurity was formidable, but it also strengthened Chinese nationalism and emboldened the government in its relentless quest for power. Moreover, despite the diplomatic revolution of the early 1970s, despite the collapse of the Soviet Union, and despite over two decades of relative peace, this sense of insecurity has not subsided. With the Party having tied its legitimacy to the reunification of the motherland, it has witnessed with great frustration that the United States continued to shield Taiwan, that it strengthened its security ties with Japan, and that it intervened robustly in the South China Sea. In spite of over four decades of growth, China is still not satisfied with its economic power, with its position in the league of fragile middle-income countries, and with many of its industries still not able to compete with their foreign peers. As much as China's security aspirations are a result of its interaction with the other powers, its economic aspirations are the result of the sense of inferiority with regard to the rich and a clear lesson from history that security only comes with prosperity. It is also difficult to consider China's aspirations unjust. Like much of the developed world in the past, it is undergoing its transition from a rural society to an urban society under a political system that is not democratic. Like much of the developed world, also, it wants to become rich and resorts to mercantilism to protect infant industries. Even many of its territorial claims and its interpretation of the international sea law are not necessarily less defensible than the interpretations of other countries.

The dilemmas that emanate from China's rise are not a matter of values and principles; they are a matter of power. The efforts of other countries to defend their position have contributed as much to that dilemma as China's efforts to improve its position. But, and this is another important finding in this work, the repercussion of China's great aspirations is that it has to alter the regional order, that it has to maximize its power to the point that it becomes the most potent player in Asia and that it can keep an eventual coalition around the United States at bay. China is seeking security through power and power to enhance its security. It is, no doubt, a revisionist power. I want to reiterate again that this study therefore does not put the blame on China. Status quo powers clinging to their primacy and privileges, like the United States, are as threatening to Asian security as a rising revisionist. It is the security dilemma between the two that causes the friction, not just China.

Hence, the changes that we discerned in China's policy are the pursuit of the same objective of power maximization with more sophisticated instruments. The goals of the revolutionary foreign policy and today's marble floor diplomacy are essentially the same, but the recent emanations of Chinese revisionism have obviously been much more efficient. In the last 20–30 years, depending on how one assesses the Taiwan Missile Crisis, China has avoided armed conflicts with its neighbors. Even in comparison to the size of its population, it has outperformed almost all its neighbors economically. It has reshaped the terms of trade with its Asian partners to its advantage, nudged many into trade deficits, and limited export opportunities mostly to raw materials. Meanwhile, the anticipated spillover of investment and manufacturing has not taken place. Rising wages notwithstanding, China has even continued to strengthen its share in labor-intensive exports. It also managed to divert an increasing part of Asia's natural richness, from fish, over ores, to water. That economic power shift has coincided with a military power shift. China is still far behind the United States, but its military modernization is impressive compared to any of its neighbors.

Looking Ahead

Quiet revisionism often proves the most effective form of revisionism, and winning the contest for Asian supremacy without fighting, as Sun Tzu would have recommended, seems exactly what China has been doing. China has made use of a combination of limited concessions, the exploitation of divisions between the other Asian countries, the cultivation of economic expectations, and massive credit lines to ward off the nightmare scenario of a neighborhood turning into a geopolitical straitjacket. So far, so good. Important in this regard is that such success has been as much the consequence of China's skillful diplomacy as the receptivity of the neighborhood for such diplomacy. That was the case already in the 1970s and it remains the case today. China's neighborhood is tough, but it is also divided, and, most importantly, multipolar. For all China's growth, it is not yet turning Asia into a bipolar or unipolar order. Smaller countries still have ample opportunity to diversify their economic relations and can do so under the American security umbrella. That is about to change, though. Countries do increasingly face the choice between resisting China and joining it.

It is thus going to be much more difficult for China to rise peacefully. The main difficulty, as we have seen, is that the neighboring countries start pushing for greater economic and political concessions, whereas the Chinese government is under growing domestic pressure not to make such concessions, and the government often assumes that it has already given enough and that many of the demands from outside are prompted by American policies of containment. This book has pointed at several factors that will add to these tensions. To begin with, contested swaths of land and sea become more crowded and often China strengthens its presence faster than other claimants. That leads not only to greater distrust, but also a greater risk of incidents. Second, China's economic model causes instability. Not only is there more criticism about Chinese policies of trade diversion and industrial nationalism; countries also become more frustrated about the unbalanced trade relations. In recent years, Beijing still appeared to be able to assuage some neighbors by offering more credit, but that did not work everywhere. Another consequence of China's emerging catch-all economy is that it prevents neighbors from developing or maintaining their own manufacturing base, limiting deficits on the current account, reducing their dependence on raw materials, constraining inflation, and creating jobs in the formal sector. That leads to dwindling satisfaction and political trust, which, in turn, leads politicians to respond with more nationalist policies and not seldom to resort to Sinophobic nationalism. This all comes at a moment when China itself is becoming less confident about the durability of its economic success and growing domestic concern about the future of the country.

At this juncture, we can see two directions in which the Asian strategic landscape might develop. If China muddles through its bottleneck and continues to outpace its neighbors, more tensions will emerge. This is especially so because we do not have any evidence that China is preparing to share more of its economic success, to make concessions in territorial disputes, or to slow down its military modernization. It is also because China's rise will take place in a context of deeply insecure and economically vulnerable neighbors, the larger one of which will have a greater tendency to resort to both nationalism and rebalancing. I do expect Beijing to invest more in its backyard when it joins the small group of high-income countries and feels more confident about the competitiveness of its industries, but that will take at least another decade. One important question arising from this is whether some of its large neighbors such as India and Japan will clench a fist before they are no longer able to do so. I think they will. To be sure, India is struggling and often failing to keep its end up. It might continue to fail, but, with Narendra Modi, firmer red lines will be drawn. Japan will certainly not tolerate any change of the territorial status quo in the East China Sea. The truth is also that those countries do not need to be entirely convinced of their strength to fight; they might be drawn into a conflict, step by step, in a way that gradually strengthens their resolve, encourages their nationalism, and makes them bolder.

If China gets stuck in its bottleneck, things for Asia could really start to look ugly. First of all, economic trouble will likely encourage Beijing to try harder to divert trade opportunities, to protect its industries, and, in other words, to beggar its neighbors. Second, it will make it more rewarding for its leaders to respond with more nationalism and to flex their muscles abroad. Third, a Chinese slowdown would lead to more social and political instability in the rest of Asia, and thus more nationalism as well. This could become particularly worrisome in the cases of Japan and Taiwan. Nothing would be more dangerous than a Taiwanese economy being pushed into uncertainty, causing the Democratic Progressive Party to return, and a Chinese government believing that the Taiwanese are both unreliable and ungrateful for its gestures.

Asia, this book concludes, is in for another tragedy of great power politics, but it is not China's tragedy alone. The Chinese leadership senses that its country is entering stormy waters. Since the arrival of a new generation of politicians, the government has gone all out to confirm its peaceful credentials, to promise more benefits, and even to work with Asia on a new development narrative that creates more opportunities. Many of those politicians and officials would truly consider it a failure if relations with Asia were to take a turn for the worse. They would also understand very well that this could presage the end of China's rejuvenation, but that is just the essence of great power tragedies: we know how the story ends, we do not like it, but are seldom able to change it. Or worse: we think we can try to change it, whereas in fact we cannot, and blame others for failing to reciprocate.

Notes

Chapter 1 Asia's China Dilemma

1 Conversation on the sidelines of the Shangri-La Dialogue, Singapore, June 11, 2011.
2 Li, Keqiang, 2013. Time for Harvest and Sowing for Future. *China Daily*, September 5, 2013.
3 Zhu, Zhiqun, 2010. *China's New Diplomacy: Rationale, Strategies and Significance.* Aldershot: Ashgate, p. 217.
4 Johnston, Alistair Ian, 2010. *Social States: China in International Institutions, 1980–2008.* Princeton, NJ: Princeton University Press, p. xxvii. For a similar argument see: Goh, Evelyn, 2013. *The Struggle for Order.* Oxford: Oxford University Press.
5 Hongyuan, Yu, 2008. *Global Warming and China's Environmental Diplomacy.* New York: Nova Science Publishers.
6 Zha, Daojiong, 2010. Oiling the Wheels of Foreign Policy? Asia Security Initiative Paper, RSIS, Singapore, March 2010.
7 The most vocal proponent of this: Qin, Yaqing, 2011. Development of International Relations Theory in China. *International Relations of the Asia Pacific*, 11, 2, 231–57.
8 Zhang, Yunling and Tang Shiping, 2007. China's Regional Strategy. In David Shambaugh, ed., *Power Shift.* Berkeley, CA: California University Press, pp. 48–68.

9 Wang, Yizhou, 2006. 和平发展阶段的国家安全 [Peace and Different Stages of Developing National Security]. 世界知识 [*World Knowledge*], October 2006.

10 Rapkin, David P. and William R. Thompson, 2006. Will Economic Interdependence Encourage China's and India's Peaceful Ascent? In Ashley J. Tellis and Michael Wills, eds., *Strategic Asia 2006–07: Trade, Interdependence, and Security*. Washington, DC: National Bureau of Asian Research, pp. 333–64.

11 Nathan, Andrew and Andrew Scobell, 2013. *China's Search for Security*. New York: Columbia University Press, p. 8. Similar argument in: Shambaugh, David, 2013. *The Partial Power: China Goes Global*. Oxford: Oxford University Press.

12 Shambaugh, David, 2013. *The Partial Power: China Goes Global*. Oxford: Oxford University Press, p. 9.

13 Friedberg, Aaron, 2011. *A Contest for Supremacy*. New York: W.W. Norton, p. 8.

14 Mearsheimer, John, 2010. The Gathering Storm: China's Challenge to US Power in Asia. *Chinese Journal of International Politics*, 3, 4, 381–96.

Chapter 2   The Revolutionary Overture

1 Fairbank, John K., 1983. *The United States and China*. Boston, MA: Harvard University Press, p. 359.

2 Lieberman, Henry, 1949. Army Dominates Communist China. *New York Times*, October 16.

3 Gluckstein, Gael, 1957. *Mao's China: Economic and Policy Survey*. London: George Allen and Unwin.

4 Heinzig, Dieter, 2004. *The Soviet Union and Communist China, 1945–1950*. New York: M.E. Sharpe, p. 101.

5 Lieberman, Henry, 1949. Population Shift Urged in Shanghai. *New York Times*, July 15.

6 Hu Feng quoted in: Hong, Zicheng, 2007. *A Century of Contemporary Chinese Literature*. Leiden: Brill, p. 75.

7 Quoted in: Qing, Simei, 2007. *From Allies to Enemies: Visions of Modernity, Identity, and U.S.–China Diplomacy, 1945–1960*. Boston, MA: Harvard University Press, p. 5.

8 Sulzberger, C.L., 1950. Vast Issues Face Peiping, Moscow. *New York Times*, January 13.

9 Baldwin, Hanson, 1949. Red Threat to Asia Gains. *New York Times*, December 18.

10 Callender, Harold, 1949. French Act to Dam the Chinese Red Tide at Indo-China Line, *New York Times*, December 11. Note: the UK recognized the PRC in January 1950.

11 Mao Zedong, 1965[1935]. On Tactics Against Japanese Imperialism. In *Selected Works of Mao Zedong*. Beijing: Foreign Language Press, vol. 1, p. 170.

12 For the Declaration, see: US Department of State, 1978. Straight Baselines: People's Republic of China. *International Boundary Study*, no. 43, July 31.

13 Mao, Zedong, 2000/1937. *On Guerrilla Warfare*. Champaign, IL: Illinois University Press, p. 89.

14 Doolin, Dennis and Robert Carver North, 1966. *The Chinese People's Republic*. Stanford, CA: Stanford University Press, p. 29.

15 Lukin, Alexander, 2003. *The Bear Watches the Dragon: Russia's Perceptions of China and the Evolution of Russian–Chinese Relations Since the Eighteenth Century*. New York: M.E. Sharpe, pp. 114–93.

16 Kramer, Mark, 1996. The USSR Foreign Ministry Appraisal of Sino–Soviet Relations on the Eve of the Split. In James Gordon Hershberg, ed., *The Cold War in Asia*. Washington, DC: Woodrow Wilson International Center for Scholars, pp. 171–2.

17 Ostermann, Christian, ed., 2008, *Bulletin: Inside China's Cold War*, Washington, DC: Woodrow Wilson International Center for Scholars, p. 245.

18 Cable for the preparation for a trade agreement with the USSR, December 22, 1949.

19 Heinzig, Dieter, *The Soviet Union and Communist China, 1945–1950*, pp. 51–107.

20 Bodde, Derk, 1950. *Peking Diary – A Year of Revolution*. New York: Henry Schuman, p. 24.

21 A very good discussion of the Chinese decision to intervene: Hao, Yufan and Zhai Zhihai, 1990. China's Decision to Enter the Korean War. *China Quarterly*, 121, 94–115.

22 Kennedy, Andrew, 2011. *The International Ambitions of Mao and Nehru*. Cambridge: Cambridge University Press, p. 86.

23 Quoted in: Xia, Yafeng, 2006. *Negotiating with the Enemy: U.S.–China Talks during the Cold War, 1949–1972*. Bloomington, IN: Indiana University Press, p. 295.

24 Tkacik, Jr., John, How the PLA Sees North Korea. In Andrew Scobell and Larry Wortzel, eds., 2006. *Shaping China's Security Environment: The Role of the People's Liberation Army*. Washington, DC: Strategic Studies Institute, p. 141.

25 William Stueck argues that Kim and Stalin had moved Mao into a position in which he could only decide to intervene. Shen Zhihua too puts much of the responsibility on Stalin. Stueck, William, 2002. *Rethinking the Korean War: A New Diplomatic and Strategic History*. Princeton, NJ: Princeton University Press; Zhihua Shen and Neil Silver (translator), 2013. *Mao, Stalin and the Korean War: Trilateral Communist Relations in the 1950s*. London: Routledge, pp. 2–9, 220. Hu Wanli even speaks of a Soviet plot to prevent Chinese influence in the Pacific. See: Hu, Wanli, 2008. *Mao's American Strategy and the Korean War*. Hamburg: VDM Verlag, p. 193.

26 The best discussion: Christensen, Thomas, 1996. *Useful Adversaries*. Princeton, NJ: Princeton University Press, pp. 100–94. Wei-Bin Zhang, 2003. *Taiwan's Modernization: Americanization and Modernizing Confucian Manifestations*. Singapore: World Scientific, p. 53; Wei, George, ed. 2012. *China–Taiwan Relations in a Global Context*. New York: Routledge.

27 Bevin, Alexander, 1992. *The Strange Connection: U.S. Intervention in China*. Westport, CT: Greenwood Press, pp. 91–121.

28 Moorsteen, Richard, 1971. *Remaking China Policy: U.S.–China Relations and Governmental Decision-making*. Santa Monica, CA: Rand Corporation, p. 91.

29 Mansourov, Alexandre, 1996. Stalin, Mao, Kim, and China's Decision to Enter the Korean War. In James Hershberg, ed. *The Cold War in Asia*. Washington, DC: Woodrow Wilson Center for International Scholars, pp. 94–107; Osterman, Christian, ed., 2007. *Bulletin: Inside China's Cold War*. Washington, DC: Woodrow Wilson International Center for Scholars.

30 Zhou, Enlai, 1968. *The Selected Works of Zhou Enlai*. Beijing: People's Press, vol. 2, p. 52.

31 Mao, Zedong, 1952/1986. Unite and Clearly Draw the Line Between the Enemy and Ourselves. In Michael Kau and John K. Leung, eds., *The Writings of Mao Zedong, 1949–1976*. New York: M.E. Sharpe, vol. 1, p. 276.

32 Ibid.

33 Quoted in Justin Lifu Lin, 2009. *Economic Development and Transition: Thought, Strategy, and Viability*. Cambridge: Cambridge University Press, p. 21.

34 Ibid., p. 23.

35 Mao, Zedong, 1945. On Coalition Government. In *Selected Works of Mao Zedong*. Beijing: Foreign Languages Press, vol. 3, p. 264.

36 Quoted in: Berding, Andrew, 1965. *Dulles on Diplomacy*. Princeton, NJ: Van Nostrand, p. 134.

37 Black, Conrad, 2007. *Richard Nixon: A Life in Full*. New York: Public Affairs, p. 291.

38 Hershberg, *The Cold War in Asia*, p. 17.

39 Osterman, Christian, ed., 2007. *Bulletin: Inside China's Cold War*. Washington, DC: Woodrow Wilson International Center for Scholars, p. 69.

40 Quoted in *Transaction*, September 1995, p. 133.

41 Reds Support Parley on Cambodia. *New York Times*, August 29, 1962.

42 Topping, Seymour, 1964. Peking Attacks Tokyo Hostility. *New York Times*, December 9, 1964.

43 Kelemen, Paul, 1984. Soviet Strategy in Southeast Asia: The Vietnam Factor. *Asian Survey*, 24, 3, 335–48.

44 For a good assessment of the different explanations: Xu, Zhangdaiwei, 2012. *Mao's Grand Strategy behind the 1958 Kinmen Shelling*. Washington, DC: Georgetown University; Jun, Niu, 2009. A Further Discussion of Decision-Making in the 1958 Shelling of Jinmen. *Journal of Modern Chinese History*, 3, 2, 147–64.

45 Zhai, Qiang, 2000. *China and the Vietnam Wars*. Chapel Hill, NC: University of North Carolina Press, p. 162.

46 Grose, Peter, 1968. US Officials Urge Chinese Reds to End Isolation. *New York Times*, May 22.

Chapter 3   The Normalization

1 Xia, Yafeng, 2006. *Negotiating with the Enemy: U.S.–China Talks during the Cold War*. Bloomington, IN: Indiana

University Press, pp. 162–89; Holdridge, John, 1997. *Crossing the Divide: An Insider's Account of Normalization of U.S.–China Relations*. Lanham, MD: Rowman and Littlefield, pp. 45–81.

2 Asian Parley Ends with Acceptance of Peking on Rise. *New York Times*, June 17, 1972.

3 Chŏng, Chae-ho, 2007. *Between Ally and Partner: Korea–China Relations and the United States*. New York: Columbia University Press, pp. 30–1.

4 Eto, Shinkichi, 1980. Recent Developments in Sino-Japanese Relations. *Asian Survey*, 20, 7, 726–43; Mackerras, Colin and Amanda Yorke, 2008. *The Cambridge Handbook of Contemporary China*. Cambridge: Cambridge University Press, p. 33.

5 Tiny Isles in Pacific Make Big Waves. *New York Times*, July 12, 1972.

6 Weng, Qingxin, 2000. *Hegemonic Cooperation and Conflict: Postwar Japan's China Policy and the United States*. Westport, CT: Praeger, pp. 179–221.

7 Li, Jinming and Li Dexia, 2003. The Dotted Line on the Chinese Map of the South China Sea. *Ocean Development & International Law*, 34, 2, 287–95.

8 Tiny Isles in Pacific Make Big Waves. *New York Times*, July 12, 1972.

9 China Says Relics Prove Isles' Past. *New York Times*, December 8, 1974.

10 Butterfield, Fox, 1975. China Reasserts Claim to Islands. *New York Times*, November 27.

11 Middleton, Drew, 1978. Soviet–Vietnamese Treaty May Alter Sea Strategies. *New York Times*, November 8.

12 Mancall, Marc, 1986. *China at the Center*. New York: The Free Press, p. 437; Four Indian Soldiers Reported Slain in China Border Clash. *Los Angeles Times*, November 2, 1975.

13 FitzGerald, Stephen, 1971. Impressions of China's New Diplomacy. *China Quarterly*, 48, 670–6.

14 Deng, Xiaoping, 1994. *Deng Xiaoping's Selected Works: Volume 3*. Beijing: People's Publishing House, p. 141.

15 Reardon, Lawrence, 1998. Learning How to Open the Door: A Reassessment of China's "Opening" Strategy. *China Quarterly*, 155, 479–511.

16 Quoted in Worden, Robert, 1983. China's Balancing Act: Cancun, the Third World, Latin America. *Asian Survey*, 23, 5, 619–36.

17 Interview with Wu Xueqian: No Soviet Cooperation. *Far Eastern Economic Review*, November 17, 1983, p. 136.

18 Deng, Xiaoping, 1994. *Deng Xiaoping's Selected Works: Volume 3*. Beijing: People's Publishing House, p. 341.

19 Deng, Xiaoping, 1994. *Deng Xiaoping's Selected Works: Volume 2*. Beijing: People's Publishing House, p. 226.

20 Zhuang Qubing, Zhang Hongzeng and Pan Tongwen, 1981. 评美国的与台湾关系法 [Criticism of the US–Taiwan Relations Act], 国际问题研究 [*Journal of International Studies*], January, p. 25.

21 Thanks to one of the reviewers for making this point.

22 Gurtov, Melvin and Byong-Moo Hwang, 1998. *China's Security: The New Roles of the Military*. London: Lynne Rienner, p. 163.

23 Quoted in Liu, Bih-Rong, 1986. *China as a Nuclear Power*. Charlottesville, VA: University of Virginia, p. 81.

24 Peng, Guangqian, 1997. The Strategic Thought of Deng Xiaoping. In Michael Pillsbury, ed., *Chinese Views of Future Warfare*. Washington, DC: National Defense University, pp. 4–18.

25 Interview with Wang, Chuanbi and others, 1987. 展望年的日本形势 [Outlook of the Situation in Japan]. 现代国际关系 [*Contemporary International Relations*], January.

26 Liangjie Jun and Lin Haohui, 1985. 拉吉夫大选获胜的背景及其施政趋向 [Rajiv's Election Victory, Its Background and Policy Trends]. 现代国际关系 [*Contemporary International Relations*], January; Hua, Biyun, 1989. 印度经济发展的成就与前景 [Achievements and Prospects of the Indian Economy]. 现代国际关系 [*Contemporary International Relations*], October; Vertzberger, Yaacov, 1982. India's Border Conflict with China: A Perceptual Analysis. *Journal of Contemporary History*, 17, 4, 607–31.

27 Wu, Zhisheng, 1984. 对东盟国家经济发展的一些看法 [Some Observations of the Economic Development of the ASEAN Countries]. 国际问题研究 [*International Studies*], October.

28 Zhou, Zhixian and Zhen Xida, 1983. 关于中国国家力量的几点看法 [Opinions on China's National Strength].

现代国际关系 [*Contemporary International Relations*],
May.

29 Yahuda, Michael, 1989. The People's Republic of China
at 40: Foreign Relations. *The China Quarterly*, no. 119,
519–39.

30 Brantly, Womack, 1994. Sino-Vietnamese Border Trade: The
Edge of Normalization. *Asian Survey*, 34, 6, 495–512.

31 Goodman, David, 1988. *Communism and Reform in East
Asia*. Abingdon: Routledge, p. 137; Kornberg, Judith and
John Faust, 2005. *China in World Politics*. West Mall, Van-
couver: University of British Columbia Press, p. 106.

32 China was one of the 23 founding members of GATT and
became a contracting party in 1948. The Kuomintang government withdrew from the GATT in 1950. In 1982, China
was granted observer status in GATT. In June 1986, China
requested "resumption" of its contracting party status.

33 Nakasone to Seek ASEAN Views on China Move. *The Straits
Times*, March 28, 1983.

34 Woods, Lawrence, 1990. Delicate Diplomatic Debuts:
Chinese and Soviet Participation in the Pacific Economic
Cooperation Conference. *Pacific Affairs*, 63, 2, 210–27.

35 China hadiri sidang Asean. *Berita Harian*, June 2, 1985.

36 D'Hooghe, Ingrid, 1994. Regional Economic Integration in
Yunnan. In David Goodman and Gerald Segal, eds., *China
Deconstructs*. Abingdon: Routledge, p. 300.

37 Unctadstat: Inward and Outward Foreign Direct Investment
Flows, Annual, 1970–2012.

Chapter 4   Briefcase Revisionism

1 Erlanger, Steven, 1989. Asian Allies Back US China Policy.
New York Times, July 8.

2 Takamine, Tsukasa, 2006. *Japan's Development Aid to
China*. Abingdon: Routledge, p. 186; Kesavan, K.V., 1990.
Japan and the Tiananmen Square Incident: Aspects of the
Bilateral Relationship. *Asian Survey*, 30, 7, 669–81.

3 Ministry of Foreign Affairs of the People's Republic of China,
Towards a Good-Neighborly Partnership of Mutual Trust
Oriented to the 21st Century. Speech given by President
Jiang Zemin at the First Summit of ASEAN, China, Japan
and ROK, December 16, 1997.

4 Premier Zhu Rongji Attending the Summit between ASEAN, China, Japan and Korea and Issuing an Important Speech. *China Daily*, November 21, 2000.

5 Interview, Singapore, January 28, 2008.

6 Interview, Singapore, January 27, 2008.

7 UNCTAD Statistics, Merchandise Trade Index.

8 Another US$69 billion flew in via Hong Kong, but a large part of that was related to so-called roundtripping. OECD, 2000. Main Determinants and Impacts of Foreign Direct Investment on China's Economy. OECD Working Papers on International Investment, 2000/04, Paris: OECD; Thais may invest $626m in China. *The Straits Times*, May 21, 1993.

9 Gill, Bates and James Reilly, 2000. Sovereignty, Intervention and Peacekeeping: The View from Beijing. *Survival*, 42, 3, 41–59.

10 Sebastian, Leonard, 2000. Southeast Asian Perceptions of China. In Derek Da Chunha, ed., *Southeast Asian Perspectives on Security*. Singapore: ISEAS, p. 169.

11 China's Tacit Disapproval. *The Straits Times*, August 18, 1989.

12 China and Laos Resume Party-to-Party Ties. *The Straits Times*, August 17, 1989.

13 Plans for Airfield in Northern Laos. *The Business Times*, August 7, 1990.

14 Foot, Rosemary, 1998. China in the ASEAN Regional Forum: Organizational Processes and Domestic Modes of Thought. *Asian Survey*, 38, 5, 425–40; Withing, Allen, 1997. ASEAN Eyes China: The Security Dimension. *Asian Survey*, 37, 4, 299–322; Lee, Tai To, 1993. ASEAN–PRC Political and Security Cooperation: Problems, Proposals, and Prospects. *Asian Survey*, 33, 1, 1095–104.

15 Luo, Shaohong, Cheng Bifan and Gao Tiesan, 1989. China's Changing Industrial Structure. In Siow Yue Chia and Bifan Cheng, eds., *ASEAN–China Economic Relations: Developments in ASEAN and China*. Singapore: ISEAS, pp. 27–34; Dao, Shulin, 1989. 重振西南丝路, 加强同南部邻国的经济联系 [Revive the Southwest Silk Road to Strengthen Economic Relations with the Southern Neighbors]. 现代国际关系 [*Contemporary International Relations*], December.

16 Chen, Jie, 1994. China's Spratly Policy: With Special Reference to the Philippines and Malaysia. *Asian Survey*, 34, 10, 893–903.

17 Joyner, Christopher, 1998. The Spratly Islands Dispute in the South China Sea: Problems, Policies, and Prospects for Diplomatic Accommodation. Washington, DC: Stimson Center, p. 67.

18 Lio, Joseph Chinyong, Strategic and Security Patterns in Malaysia's Relations with China. In Ho Khai Leong and Samuel Ku, eds., *China and Southeast Asia: Global Changes and Regional Challenges*. Singapore: ISEAS, p. 292.

19 Chen, Jie, 1994. China's Spratly Policy: With Special Reference to the Philippines and Malaysia. *Asian Survey*, 34, 10, 893–903.

20 Teufel Dreyer, June, 1990. Taiwan in 1989: Democratization and Economic Growth. *Asian Survey*, 30, 1, 52–8.

21 Taiwan's 4-Point Plan on Dealing with China. *The Straits Times*, June 15, 1989.

22 The 8-Point Proposition Made by President Jiang Zemin on China's Reunification, January 30, 1995.

23 Conversation with Japanese diplomat posted in Beijing at the time of the visit. Brussels, October 20, 2011.

24 Bong, Younshik, 2002. *Flashpoints at Sea?* Philadelphia, PA: University of Pennsylvania, p. 61.

25 A very good discussion of these negotiations can be found in Kuhrt, Natasha, 2007. *Russian Policy towards China and Japan*. Abingdon: Routledge, pp. 28–45.

26 Chung, Chien-peng, 2003. *Domestic Politics, International Bargaining and China's Territorial Disputes*. London: Routledge, p. 199.

27 Erlanger, Steven, 1992. Yeltsin Cuts Visit to Beijing Short. *New York Times*, December 19.

28 Kristof, Nicholas, 1991. China; Beijing Backs Away From Full Support of the War. *New York Times*, February 1.

29 Russian–Chinese Joint Declaration on a Multipolar World and the Establishment of a New International Order, Moscow, April 23, 1997.

30 Conversation, Beijing, November 22, 2009.

31 For the full text of the China–Mongolia 1994 Treaty, see *Mongolian Defence White Paper, 1997–1998*, n. 19, pp. 93–5.

32 Wu, John, 1998. *The Mineral Industry of Mongolia*. Washington, DC: USGS.
33 Nichol, James, 1995. *Diplomacy in the Former Soviet Republics*. Westport, CT: Praeger, p. 165.
34 Melet, Yasmin, 1998. China's political and economic relations with Kazakhstan and Kyrgyzstan. *Central Asian Survey*, 17, 2, 229–52.
35 Quoted in Wang, Jisi, 2011. China's Search for a Grand Strategy, *Foreign Affairs*, 90, 2, 68–79.
36 Chinese President Jiang Zemin delivered a keynote speech at the dinner for the opening of the Fortune Global Forum 2001 in Hong Kong, May 8; see: http://www.fmprc.gov.cn/eng/wjdt/zyjh/t25025.htm.

Chapter 5   Peaceful Development

1 Between 1989 and 2002, Southeast Asia grew on average by 6 percent, its consumer price index by 11 percent.
2 Injecting Fresh Vigor into World Economy, *People's Daily*, October 17, 2001.
3 Eckholm, Erik, 2001. China's Inner Circle Reveals Big Unrest, and Lists Causes, *New York Times*, June 3. See also Perry, Elisabeth, 1999. *Challenging the Mandate of Heaven*. New York: M.E. Sharpe.
4 Wang, Yizhou, 2009. Transition of China's Diplomacy and Foreign Relations. *China and World Economy*, 17, 3, 93–102.
5 Zhang Boli, 2000. 经济全球化是一把"双刃剑" [Globalization is a Double-Edged Sword]. *People's Daily*, March 30.
6 Ministry of Defence, Japan, 2001. *Defence of Japan*. Tokyo: Ministry of Defence.
7 Department of Defense, 2001. *Quadrennial Defense Review Report*. Washington, DC: Department of Defense, p. 20; White House, 2002. *The National Security Strategy of the United States of America*. Washington, DC: White House, p. 9.
8 Jiang, Zemin, 1999. Speech at the Conference on Disarmament. Geneva, March 26.
9 PNAC, 2000. *Rebuilding America's Defenses: Strategy, Forces and Resources for a New Century*. Washington, DC: Project for the New American Century.

10 Beijing Six-Party Talks Highlight China's Role. *People's Daily*, August 30, 2003.

11 Shirk, Susan L., 2007. *China: Fragile Superpower*. New York: Oxford University Press, p. 112.

12 Interview with official, Jakarta, January 19, 2008.

13 Interview with expert, Beijing, October 12, 2010.

14 Note verbale of the PRC to the UN Secretary General, CML/18/2009, May 7, 2009.

15 Beckman, Robert and Tara Davenport, 2010. *CLCS Submissions and Claims in the South China Sea*. Singapore: National Law University.

16 Declaration on the Conduct of Parties in the South China Sea, November 4, 2002, art. 5.

17 By far the best overview: Thayer, Carlyle, 2012. Building ASEAN'S Code of Conduct in the South China Sea: A Litmus Test for Community? *Asia-Pacific Journal*, 34, 4.

18 In 2010, a ship-based helicopter flight was confirmed in waters approximately 260 kilometers northeast of Okinotorishima.

19 Conversation with Chinese official, Brussels, March 4, 2013.

20 http://ebas1.ebas.gov.tw/pxweb/Dialog/statfile1L.asp.

21 Shu, Chulong and Guo Yuli, 2008. Change: Mainland's Taiwan Policy. *China Security*, 4, 1, 127–33.

22 Wong, Edward, 2008. Taiwan and China Draw Closer with New Agreements. *New York Times*, November 4.

23 Mainland Affairs Council, 2010. Cross-Strait Economic Statistics Monthly, no. 210, Table 20.

24 President Hu Visits Taiwan Businesses on Mainland ahead of Spring Festival. *People's Daily*, February 13, 2010.

25 For the agreement, see the Taiwanese Ministry of Economic Affairs: http://www.moea.gov.tw/Mns/populace/news/News.aspx?kind=1&menu_id=40&news_id=19723.

26 Chinese Procurement in Taiwan Tops US$15 Billion in 2010, *Financial Times*, September 29, 2010.

27 Report on ASEAN–China Economic and Trade Seminar, Beijing, January 25–28, 2013.

28 Zhang, Yunling, 2004. China's Economic Emergence and its Impact, China Academy of Social Sciences, Beijing, March 10.

29 Zhang, Xiaoji, 2000. Ways Towards East Asian FTA. In Saw Swee-Hock, Sheng Lijun, and Chin Kin Wah, eds., *ASEAN–China Relations: Realities and Prospects*. Singapore: Institute of Southeast Asian Studies, p. 80.
30 Ibid., p. 72; Dialogue: Pan-Beibu Gulf Economic Cooperation under East-Asia Cooperation Framework, available at http://www.cafta.org.cn/show.php?contentid=61415.
31 Jia, Heping, 2003. US-Singaporean FTA to Affect Bloc Talks. *China Business Weekly*, May 20. See also: Yang, Hongjiang and Liang Wu, 2006. Meiguo ziyou maoyi xieding zhanlue anpai yu zhongguo jingzheng diwei yanjiu [Study on America Free Trade Agreement Strategy and China's Competition Status], *Xiandai caijing* [*Modern Finance and Economics*], January.
32 China Welcomes Import from ASEAN Despite Trade Deficit. *China Daily*, November 3, 2006.
33 Zhang, Haibing, 2007. China's Aid to Southeast Asia. In Swee-Hock Saw, ed., *ASEAN–China Economic Relations*. Singapore: Institute of Southeast Asian Studies, pp. 256–62.
34 CEPA, arts 1 and 2.
35 Protest did occur in Thailand over Chinese "dumping" of onions and garlic, but these frustrations were offset by the positive expectations created among other ASEAN members.
36 Conversation, Brussels, June 23, 2013.

Chapter 6   Elusive Harmony

1 Jun, Xiao, 2010. ASEAN–China FTA: A Pragmatic Approach to Regulating Services and Investment. In Philippe Gugler and Julien Chaisse, eds., *Competitiveness of the ASEAN Countries: Corporate and Regulatory Drivers*. New York: Edward Elgar, pp. 237–59.
2 World Development Indicators Database, Council on Tall Buildings and Urban Habitat Statistics, and UNCTAD Review of Maritime Transport.
3 Pew Global Attitudes Project Database. Is the Country's Economic Situation Good or Bad? And How Satisfied Are You with the Country's Direction?

4 Euromonitor, 2012. *Consumer Asia Pacific and Australasia.* London: Euromonitor.

5 UN Comtrade Database with China's partners as reporters. See: http://comtrade.un.org/.

6 FDI stock: MOFCOM, 2013. Statistical Bulletin of China's Outward Direct Investment. Beijing: Mofcom; UNCTAD Statistical Database. See: http://unctad.org/en/pages/Statistics.aspx.

7 Bank of Japan, 2013. *International Investment Position of Japan (Assets).*

8 SIPRI Military Expenditure Database, 2014. *Military Expenditure by Country.* Stockholm: Stockholm International Peace Research Institute.

9 Zhou, Yang, 俄称中国王牌飞行员年飞180小时接近世界一流 [Russia Reports that China's 180 Flying Hours Is World Class], *Huanqiu Ribao*, January 13, 2014; 媒体称我空军飞行员年飞小时数达200接近美军 [Media: Air Force Pilots' Flight Hours Approach US], *Xinhua*, February 7, 2012.

10 This represents about one third of China's official budget: Cheung, Tai-Ming, ed., 2013. *The Chinese Defense Economy Takes Off.* San Diego, CA: University of California Institute on Global Conflict and Cooperation.

Chapter 7   Economic Power

1 World Development Indicators. See: http://data.worldbank.org/data-catalog/world-development-indicators.

2 Sasada, Hironori, 2006. Youth and Nationalism in Japan. *SAIS Review of International Affairs*, 26, 2, 109–22; Honda, Yuki, 2007. Review Essay Focusing in on Contemporary Japan's "Youth" Nationalism. *Social Science Japan Journal*, 10, 2, 281–6.

3 On patriotism and age, see World Value Survey Database, "Willingness to Fight for the Country." See: http://www.worldvaluessurvey.org/WVSContents.jsp.

4 Vu, Tuong, 2013. *Searching for a New Consensus and Bracing for New Conflicts: The Politics of Nationalism in Contemporary Vietnam.* Paper presented at the ANU College of Asia, Canberra, December.

5 China's Diplomacy Serves Economy. *China Daily*, March 7, 2009.
6 China to Focus on Common Interests in Economic Diplomacy. *People's Daily*, March 23, 2008.
7 Development and Research Commission World Economic and Trade Patterns Task Force, 2013. 全球化未来趋势及对我国的影响 [*The Future Trends of Globalization and their Impact on China*]. Beijing: DRC, June 13.
8 Liao, Jia, 2013. 企业开拓新兴市场将获政策支持七部门联合发文, Seven Departments Issued a Joint Policy Document to Support Companies to Expand in Emerging Markets. 经济参考报 *Economic Information Daily*, May 10; Ministry of Commerce, 2013. "外贸结构调整"专题新闻发布会 Foreign Trade Structure Adjustment Special Press Conference. Beijing, Ministry of Commerce, May 9.
9 Miao Wei, 2014. 在全面深化改革中打造制造业强国 [*Advancing Industrial Power in the Context of Overall Deepening Reforms*]. *Qiushi*, March 1; State Council, 2013. 政府工作报告: 对今年政府工作的建议 [Government Work Report: Proposal for 2013 Work]. Beijing: State Council, March 18, section 1.2.
10 Ren Zeping, 2013. 任泽平：我国制造业发展的现状与趋势 [Development Status and Trends of China's Manufacturing Industry]. *Economic Daily*, August 6.
11 Xuan, Xiaowei, 2013. 宣晓伟：中国迈向高收入: 发展方式转变和现代化转型 [China Towards High Income Status: Development Mode Transformation and Modernization], 中国发展观察, *China Development Observer*, June; Interview with Chen Changsheng, Vice Minister and Research Fellow DRC: Lu, Hongxing, 2013. 陈昌盛:我国经济已步入增长阶段转换的关键期 [Chen Changsheng: China's Economy Has Entered a Critical Period of Growth Adjustment]. *China Economic Times*, August 9.
12 DRC World Economic and Trade Patterns Task Force, 2013. 全球化未来趋势及对我国的影响 [*The Future Trends of Globalization and their Impact on China*]. Beijing: DRC, June 13; Ministry of Finance, 2013. 中国资产评估行业发展规划 [*An Evaluation of China's Industrial Assets Development Plan*]. Beijing: Ministry of Finance, April 25, section 1.
13 State Council, 2013. 政府工作报告: 对今年政府工作的建议 [*Government Work Report: Proposal for 2013 Work*].

Beijing: State Council, March 18, section 1; State Council, 2013. "十二五"国家自主创新能力建设规划 [Twelfth Five-year National Innovation Capacity-Building Program]. Beijing: State Council; Gua-Fa, no. 4, January 2013, section 1.4; Ministry of Finance, 2013. 关于编报2014年中央国有资本经营预算建议草案的通知 [*Notice Concerning the 2014 Budget for the National State-Owned Companies*]. Beijing: Ministry of Finance, July, sections 1, 2.2.

14 Miao Wei, 2014. 在全面深化改革中打造制造业强国 [Advancing Industrial Power in the Context of Overall Deepening Reforms]. *Qiushi*, March 1.

15 Interview with Long Guoqiang, Senior Research Fellow and Director-General, Research Department, Foreign Economic Relations: Lu, Hongxing, 2013; 隆国强：我国应实行动态比较优势的出口升级战略 [Long Guoqiang: China Should Implement a Strategy to Dynamically Upgrade the Competitive Advantages of its Exports], *China Economic Times*, July 17.

16 Calculated as follows: export of manufactured goods minus imports of manufactured goods divided by total manufacturing output. Source: World Development Indicators and UN Comtrade.

17 NDRC, 2014. Report on the Implementation of the 2013 Plan for National Economic and Social Development and on the 2014 Draft Plan for National Economic and Social Development. Beijing: NDRC, p. 16.

18 Liao, Jia, 2013. 企业开拓新兴市场将获政策支持七部门联合发文, Seven Departments Issued a Joint Policy Document to Support Companies to Expand in Emerging Markets. 经济参考报 *Economic Information Daily*, May 10; Ministry of Commerce, 2013. "外贸结构调整"专题新闻发布会 Foreign Trade Structure Adjustment Special Press Conference. Beijing, Ministry of Commerce, May 9.

19 Ministry of Commerce, 2013. "外贸结构调整"专题新闻发布会 Foreign Trade Structure Adjustment Special Press Conference. Beijing, Ministry of Commerce, May 9; 中国工程机械出口东南亚分析 [Analysis of Construction Equipment Exports to Southeast Asia]. *MOFCOM*, June 19, 2012, http://ccn.mofcom.gov.cn/spbg/show.php?id=13113.

20 Total outward direct investments divided by GDP. Data for 2012. Source: UNCTADStats.

21 Statement by Mr. Yukio Edano, Minister of Economy, Trade and Industry at the Opening Plenary of the 8th Session of the WTO Ministerial Conference, Geneva, December 15, 2011.

22 Ministry of Commerce, 2012. 对外贸易发展"十二五"规划 [*Foreign Trade Development and the Twelfth Five Year Plan*]. Beijing: Ministry of Commerce, April 26, 4.3. See also: International Research Institute of the NDRC, 2013. 我国境外投资出现战略布局新窗口 [China's Strategy for Foreign Investment Abroad Becomes a New Window of Opportunity]. *MOFCOM*, June 6.

23 Jiang, Julie and Jonathan Sinton, 2012. *Overseas Investments by Chinese National Oil Companies*. Paris: International Energy Agency, p. 9.

24 US Geological Survey reports for the Asia-Pacific: http://minerals.usgs.gov/minerals/pubs/country/asia.html#cb.

25 Cheng, Guoqiang, 2014. 境外农业资源利用的现状与问题 [Status and Problems of the Use of Foreign Agricultural Resources]. State Council Development Research Center, January 21; Fang, Zhengqiang, 2011. 我国粮食安全问题不容忽视 [Our Food Security Problems Cannot be Ignored]. *Xinhua* and *Qiushi*, November 29; Ministry of Agriculture, 2011. 农业国际合作发展十二五规划 [*Agricultural International Cooperation and Development in the Twelfth Five-Year Plan*]. Beijing: Ministry of Agriculture.

26 Wang, Chengyue, 2013. 中国农业走出去出路在哪里 [Can Agricultural Going Abroad Offer a Way Out?]. *China Economic Weekly*, December 24.

27 Bruzelius Backer, Ellen, 2007. The Mekong River Commission: Does It Work, and How Does the Mekong Basin's Geography Influence Its Effectiveness? *Südostasien aktuell*, 31, 4, 31–55; Bakker, Karen, 1999. The Politics of Hydropower: Developing the Mekong. *Political Geography*, 18, 1, 209–32.

28 南水北调西线工程：个别省份意见强烈 尚难动工 [Western Route Project: Different Provinces Advise to Start with Vigour]. *Xinhua*, November 19, 2013. See also the webpage of the South–North Project: 中国南水北调: www.nsbd.gov.cn.

29 A very good background article: Zhanglu Jing, 2013. 蛟龙号绘制中国深海藏宝图1.1万米版引进民资　[Chinese

Dragon Finds Treasure at 11,000 Meters Deep]. 中国经济周刊 [*China Economic Weekly*], December 24. China has developed a first small platform for deep-sea mining, the Dragon. See: 蛟龙号再次深潜探索深海采矿可能性 [Another Diving Expedition of the Dragon to Explore the Possibilities of Sea-Mining]. 东方早报 [*Oriental Morning Post*], August 9, 2013.

30 习近平:开展海洋和极地考察具有重大现实意义 [Xi Jinping: Conducting Ocean and Polar Expeditions is of Great Practical Importance]. *Xinhua*, June 21, 2013.

31 Davison, Nicola, 2013. China Eyes Antarctica's Resource Bounty. *The Guardian*, November 8.

32 International Monetary Institute, Renmin University of China, 2014. *The Internationalization of the Renminbi*. Abingdon: Routledge, p. 8.

33 Yukon, Huang, 2013. Does Internationalizing the RMB Make Sense for China? *Cato Journal*, 33, 3, 571–85.

34 Quoted in Wright, Chris, 2013. Ex-Regulator Plays Down Yuan Reserve Currency Role. *Emerging Markets*, May 2, available at: http://www.emergingmarkets.org/Article/3200130/Ex-regulator-plays-down-Renminbi-reserve-currency-role.html.

Chapter 8   The Contest for the Pacific

1 Conversations during Chinese state visit, Brussels, April 1–2, 2014.

2 Nian, Lingyun, 2012. 论日本加剧钓鱼岛争端的原因 [The Causes of the Intensified Conflict with Japan over the Diaoyu Islands]. 科技视界 [*Science & Technology Vision*], 29, 7–15; Wen, Jiang, 2012. 钓鱼岛争端将加剧日本内外交困 [The Dispute with Japan over the Diaoyu Islands Will Exacerbate because of the Downturn]. 小康 [*China Insight*], 97–8.

3 两岸多数民众支持保钓 [Taiwan and Mainland Poll Shows Majority Willing to Defend Diaoyu Islands]. *Global Times*, July 19, 2012. See also: How to Defend the Diaoyu Islands Most Effectively? http://survey.inewsweek.cn/vote_result.php?vote_id=158.

4 Review of 2013 papers in 台湾研究集刊 [*Taiwan Research Quarterly*], the most important mainland journal on

Taiwanese affairs. See also the opinions of one of the leading specialists on the subject: Chen, Kongli, 2014. 破解两岸难题需要什么样的想象力 [What Kind of Imagination We Need to Crack the Cross-Straits Problem]. *Xinhua*, February 17.

5 For example: Zhong, Yu, 2012. 2012年台湾政局暨两岸关系回顾与展望"研讨会在京召开 [Seminar Held in Beijing on Review and Outlook of Taiwan's 2012 Election and the Cross-Straits Relations]. *Xinhua*, December 5.

6 Dua, Nusa, 2013. China's Xi Says Political Solution for Taiwan Can't Wait Forever. Reuters, October 6.

7 Chang, Jun, 2013. Fresh New Ideas Urged on Taiwan Issue. *China Daily*, November 4.

8 Conversation with Chinese official, Beijing, December 21, 2012.

9 70%的网友支持中国在南海动武 [70% of Netizens Support China's Use of Force in South China Sea]. Qian Zhan, July 6, 2012, available at: http://www.qianzhan.com/indynews/detail/256/121218-ad23da8a.html.

10 国家安全与军费开支的国民见解 [National Opinion Poll on the National Security and Military Spending], March 20, 2014.

11 SIPRI Military Expenditure Database: Comparison of Averages for 2005–2008 and 2009–2012: Vietnam from 2.2 to 2.4 percent, South Korea from 2.7 to 2.8 percent, India from 2.5 to 2.7 percent.

12 Xi Jinping, 2013. 习近平在莫斯科国际关系学院的演讲 [Speech at the Moscow Institute of International Affairs], March 24. See also: Xi, Jinping, 2013. 习近平在博鳌亚洲论坛2013年会上的主旨演讲 [Xi Jinping Keynote Speech for the Bao Forum Asia 2013 Conference], April 7.

13 Liu, Jianfei and Zuo Fengrong, 2013. 世界乱象背后的基本大势 [The Main Trends Behind the Global Turbulence]. 当代世界 [*Contemporary World*], August.

14 Xuanxing Zhang, 2013. 正在浮现的世界新秩序 [The Emerging World Order]. 当代世界 [*Contemporary World*], December.

15 Zuo, Fengrong, 2014. 大国力量更趋平衡和平发展大势所趋 [Major Power Rebalancing and the Trend of Peace]. 当代世界 [*Contemporary World*], January.

16 Zhao, Jin, 2012. 中国崛起与周边地缘战略依托 [China's Rise and its Geostrategic Dependence on its Neighborhood]. 当代世界 [*Contemporary World*], October.

17 Tao, Wenzhao, 2014. 中美新型大国关系重在落实 [Focusing on the Development of the New Sino–US Major Powers Partnership]. 当代世界 [*Contemporary World*], January. See also: Su, Xiaohui and Cheng Lung, 2013. 当前国际形势的几个新动向 [Various New Trends in the Current International Situation]. 当代世界 [*Contemporary World*], August.

18 Chief Researcher of the Marine Research Center: Li Jie, 2013. 美加速构建第二岛链"桥头堡" [The United States Accelerated Construction of a Second Island Chain "Bridgehead"], September 30. See also: Tao, Wenzhao, 2014. 中美新型大国关系重在落实 [Focusing on the Development of the New Sino–US Major Powers Partnership]. 当代世界 [*Contemporary World*], January; Su, Xiaohui and Cheng Lung, 2013. 当前国际形势的几个新动向 [Various New Trends in the Current International Situation]. 当代世界 [*Contemporary World*], August.

19 Han, Xudong, 2011. 美国在逼中国加速提升军力 [America Compels China to Accelerate Its Military Modernization]. *People's Daily*, June 1.

20 Yang, Yi, 2011. 空海一体战与世界潮流背道而驰 [Air-Sea Battle Contradicts the Global Trend]. *People's Daily*, December 12; Cheng, Guilong, 2013. 论"空海一体战"与中国国家安全 [On Air-Sea Battle and China's National Security] 国防科技 [*Defence Science and Technology*], 5, 59–65.

21 Huangzai Juan and Li Yang, 2013. 分析：日本急欲采购的七种武器究竟成色如何? [Analysis: How about the Quality of the Seven Weapons Japan Is Anxious to Procure?]. *People's Daily*, March 22.

22 Wu, Qin, 2014. 航母杀手来袭 [Aircraft Killer to Strike]. *Military Digest*, January.

23 Wen, Xian et al., 2012. 空海一体战折射军事战略变化 [Air-Sea Battle Reflects Changes in Military Strategy]. *People's Daily*, February 27; Yang, Yi, 2011. 空海一体战与世界潮流背道而驰 [Air-Sea Battle Contradicts the Global Trend]. *People's Daily*, December 12.

24 Li, Jie, 2014. 警惕美"空海一体战"升级变异 [Wary of the United States "Air Sea Battle," Upgrading Variation], January 14.

25 Seven destroyers of the 15th squadron at Yokosuka and six Japanese destroyers.

26 Li, Jie, 2014. 警惕美"空海一体战"升级变异 [Wary of the United States "Air Sea Battle," Upgrading Variation], January 14; 美在日部署P8巡逻机 欲对中国舰艇动态"了如指掌" [P8 patrol aircraft deployed by the United States in Japan with the aim to know Chinese warship movements "like the back of their hand"]. 中国日报网 [China Daily], February 20, 2013.

27 NMFS, 2007. Annual Report No. 1: Operation of the Surveillance Towed Array Sensor System Low Frequency Active (SURTASS LFA) Sonar Onboard the R/V Cory Chouest and USNS IMPECCABLE (T-AGOS 23). Washington, DC: NMFS, August 15, p. 14.

28 Beijing Daily explained that the United States and Japan are working together to establish a network of submarine cables around the Diaoyu Islands, the Ryukyu Islands and the Bashi Channel: Wei, Zheng, 2013. 美日联手在中国潜艇基地周围设置水下监听网 [United States and Japan Jointly Set Underwater Listening Network Around the Chinese Submarine Base]. 北京日报 [Beijing Daily], July 10.

29 Fengli, Qi, 2013. 美军P-8A侦察机来者不善 欲将中国核潜艇封锁在岛链内 [U.S. Military Reconnaissance Aircraft P-8A Has Ill Intent in the Island Chain in the Chinese Nuclear Submarine Blockade]? 人民日报 [People's Daily], December 12.

30 Huangzai Juan and Li Yang, 2012. 分析：日本急欲采购的七种武器究竟成色如何? [Analysis: How about the Quality of the Seven Weapons Japan Is Anxious to Procure?]. People's Daily, March 22.

31 Zhaoming, Hao, 2012. 美国亚太再平衡战略视野下的美日同盟转型 [America's Asia-Pacific Strategy Behind the US–Japan Alliance Rebalancing]. 当代世界 [Contemporary Record], October.

32 Zheng, Wenhao, 2013. 美对华海空一体战的七种武器? [A Dagger Hidden Behind Smiles: Seven Weapons for America's Air-Sea Battle against China?] 北京晚报 [Beijing Evening News], December 24.

33 Wen, Xian et al., 2012. 空海一体战折射军事战略变化 [Air-Sea Battle Reflects Changes in Military Strategy]. People's

Daily, February 27; Huang, Zhicheng, 2006. 太空武器化与太空威慑 [The Militarization of Space and Space-based Deterrence]. 国际技术经济研究 [*International Technology and Economics*], 9, 1, 24–9.

34 Deputy Secretary of Defense Speech, Press Club Washington, May 7, 2013: http://www.defense.gov/speeches/speech.aspx?speechid=1775.

35 Huangzai Juan and Li Yang, 2013. 分析：日本急欲采购的七种武器究竟成色如何? [Analysis: How about the Quality of the Seven Weapons Japan Is Anxious to Procure?]. *People's Daily*, March 22.

36 还魂"僵尸" – 美军再掀太空军备竞赛 [The Return of the Zombie: The US is Sparking another Arms Race in Space]. 军事文摘 [*Military Digest*], December 2012.

37 Li, Yunlong and Yu Xiaohong, 2013. 美军"空海一体战"空间作战行动探析 [Analysis on the US Space Operations in the "Air-Sea Battle" Concept]. 装备学院学报 [*Journal of the Academy of Equipment*], 4, 1, 81–94.

38 For instance: Wu, Xinbo, 2014. 解读美国2014版四年防务评估报告 [Interpretation of the 2014 Edition of the American Quadrennial Defense Review]. Fudan University.

39 Zhang, Junshe, 2014. 个别国家视其为遏制中国城墙 [Only One or Two Countries to Check Chinese Walls]. *PLA Daily*, February 7.

40 Ibid.

41 Ren, Weidong, 2013. 中国要实现亚太战略平衡 [China's Strategy to Reach a New Equilibrium in the Asia-Pacific]. *Xinhua*, January 30.

42 Li Xuanliang, 2012. 中国拥有航母不会改变防御性国防政策 [China's New Aircraft Carrier Will Not Change its Defensive National Defense Policy]. *Xinhua*, September 26.

43 重新定位中国近海防御战略:加大海上防御纵深 [Repositioning Chinese Coastal Defense Strategy]. *Xinhua*, July 13, 2008. See also: Peng, Guanqian, 2011. 制约战争的中国海上力量 [To Restrict Conflict We Must Aim to Expand Our Power in the China Sea]. 瞭望 [*Outlook*], August.

44 重新定位中国近海防御战略:加大海上防御纵深 [Repositioning Chinese Coastal Defense Strategy: To Increase Maritime Defense in Depth]. *Xinhua*, March 16, 2008.

45 For instance: Li, Bing and Zhu Jun, 2010. 浅析新中国海军战略思想的发展演变 [On the Evolution of the Navy

Strategic Thought of New China]. 军事历史 [*Military History*], December, 38–40; Zhang, Junshe, 2014. 个别国家视其为遏制中国城墙 [Only One or Two Countries to Check Chinese Walls]. *PLA Daily*, February 7.

46 Wang, Zaihui, 2013. 国防部:中国海军赴西太平洋训练不存在"突破"问题 [Defense Ministry: There is No Problem with China's Breakthrough in Going to the Western Pacific]. *Xinhua*, July 25; Yang Qiongte et al., 2014. 中国海军远海训练的变与不变 [Chinese Navy Distant Sea Training Changed and Unchanged]. *Xinhua*, February 11.

47 President Obama and President Xi Jinping of China deliver statements to the press before a bilateral meeting. June 7, 2013.

48 Wang, Zaihui, 2013. 国防部:中国海军赴西太平洋训练不存在"突破"问题 [Defense Ministry: There is No Problem with China's Breakthrough in Going to the Western Pacific]. *Xinhua*, July 25.

49 Kang, Yongsheng, 2013. 机动-5号展示中国海军全新训练模式 [Mobile V Shows the New Training Mode of the Navy]. *China Youth Daily*, November 8.

50 For example: Han, Xudong, 2011. 建设现代化海军 [Constructing a Modern Navy]. 瞭望 [*Outlook*], August; Li, Daguang, 2012. 中国向蓝水海军转型意义深远 [China's Profound Transformation into a Blue Water Navy]. 中国军转民 [China's Army Transformed into Civilians], December, 16–21; Shen, Zhihe and Piao Chengri, 2013. 航母编队反潜巡逻机空域配置方法研究 [A Study of the Deployment of Anti-Submarine Patrol Aircraft in Carrier Battle Group Formation]. 军事运筹与系统工程 [*Military Operations Research and System Engineering*], 21, 1, 31–40. See also: Wang, Zaihui, 2013. 国防部: 中国海军赴西太平洋训练不存在"突破"问题 [Defense Ministry: There is No Problem with China's Breakthrough in Going to the Western Pacific]. *Xinhua*, July 25.

51 Tu Chenxi, 2014. 中国航母电弹弓获重大突破 紧追美国世界第二 [China's Electromagnetic Catapult is a Major Breakthrough in Pursuit of the United States]. *People's Daily*, January 29.

52 Li, Sai et al., 2013. 远海作战装备供应链体系架构 [Architecture of High Seas Combat Equipment Supply Chain]. 国防科技 [*National Defense Science and Technology*], 35, 5,

12–20; Yang, Zhen and Du Binwei, 2013. 基于海权视角:航空母舰对中国海军转型的推动作用 [On Aircraft Carrier's Promoting Role in the Transformation of China's Naval Forces from the Perspective of Sea Power]. 太平洋学报 [*Pacific Journal*], 21, 3, 1–5.

53 Tu, Chenxin, 2013. 中国新型智能鱼雷:击沉数千吨级靶舰如捏易拉罐 [China's New Intelligent Torpedo: A Ship of Thousands of Tons Ripped Apart and Sunk]. *Xinhua*, October 23.

54 Over 40 papers on 水声探测网 [The underwater acoustic detection network], can be found in the Wanfang Database between 2001 and 2013. See: http://www.wanfangdata.com/.

55 中国在南海演练夺岛将建更多的前哨部队 [China Is About to Practice the Seizure of South China Sea Islands and Aims to Build more Military Outposts]. *Xinhua*, April 10, 2013; Guo, Xuan, 2013. 中国光纤线列阵水声探测系统令他国潜艇无所遁形 [Chinese Fibre-Optic Underwater Acoustic Submarine Detection Array Network]. 世界报 [*World News*], October 16.

56 Jianlong, Chang, Zhao Liangyu, and Like Yong, 2012. 临近空间平台与空天飞机在未来战争中的协同作用 [Synergy Between Near-Space Platforms and Space Planes in Future Wars]. 飞航导弹 [*Aerodynamic Missile Journal*], September, 81–5.

57 A good overview can be found in Easton, Ian and Mark Stokes, 2011. China's Electronic Intelligence Satellite Developments. Arlington, VA: Project 2049 Institute. Zeng, Weimin et al., 2013. 深空探测器被动式高精度多普勒测量方法与应用. [Passive Deep Space Probes and Application of High-Precision Doppler Measurements]. 宇航学报 [*Journal of Astronautics*], 31, 12; Su, Jianwei et al., 2009. 海洋监视卫星对水面舰艇电子侦察效能分析 [Electronic Reconnaissance Effectiveness Analysis of Ocean Surveillance Satellite-to-Surface Ship]. 舰船电子对抗 [*Shipboard Electronic Countermeasures*], 32, 4.

58 Zhang, Yujun and Chao Yuhua, 2011. 海洋监视卫星作战效能仿真研究 [Simulation of Operational Effectiveness of Ocean Surveillance Satellite]. 军事运筹与系统工程 [*Military Operations Research and Systems Engineering*], 25, 1, 26.

59　Feng, Zhiwei et al., 2013. 基于路径规划的敏捷卫星姿态机动反馈控制方法 [Feedback Control Method for Attitude Maneuver of Agile Satellite Based on Trajectory Optimization]. 国防科技大学学报 [*Journal of the National Defense University*], 35, 4, 2–6.

60　For example: Zhu, Jianwen, 2013. 高超声速飞行器俯冲机动最优制导方法 [The Optimal Guidance Method for Hypersonic Vehicle in Dive Phase]. 国防科技大学学报 [*Journal of the National Defense University*], 25–30; Huang, Fei et al., 2013. 连续流失效对近空间飞行器气动特性的影响 [Effects of Continuum Breakdown on Aerodynamics of Near Space Vehicle]. 空气动力学学报 [*Acta Aerodynamica Sinica*], 31, 5, 623–8.

61　Yang, Xiaojie, 2014. 中国重点型号无人空天飞机完成自主高速着陆试验 [Chinese Unmanned Space Plane Completes Important Autonomous Landing Test]. 闽南日报 [*Fujian Daily*], February 19.

62　In 2014, for instance, China expressed its concern about Japan refusing for a while to return several hundred kilos of weapons-grade plutonium to the United States. Japan reportedly has several tons of plutonium stocked and has built a new nuclear fuel plant at Rokkasho to produce more. In September 2006, the government reportedly completed an internal report assessing the possibility of producing nuclear weapons domestically.

Chapter 9　Another Great Power Tragedy

1　Conversation with senior Chinese official, Bruges, April 1, 2014.

Index